The Nest Egg Cookbook

The Nest Egg Cookbook

John Pollock

Library of Congress Control Number: 2009914263

ISBN:	Hardcover	978-1-4500-2279-8
	Softcover	978-1-4500-2278-1
	Ebook	978-1-4500-2280-4

This book was printed in the United States of America.

To order additional copies of this book, contact:
Xlibris Corporation
1-888-795-4274
www.Xlibris.com
Orders@Xlibris.com
71899

Contents

Introduction

> To invest successfully for a lifetime does not require a stratospheric IQ, unusual business insight or inside information. What's needed is a sound intellectual framework for decisions and the ability to keep emotions from corroding that framework—Warren Buffett.

Your Nest Egg is that special sum of money saved and invested for one specific future purpose—your retiremcnt. Just like the farmer that carefully watches over the eggs in the hen house, you have done what you could to save, grow, and protect your Nest Egg. Now what? Volumes have been written about creating your Nest Egg. Volumes have been written about investing your Nest Egg. But you are closing in on the day when you need to "crack" open the Nest Egg and "eat" it. Is the Nest Egg big enough? Will it last your lifetime? If it isn't big enough, how do you grow it while using it? You need a recipe for retirement success. You need a Nest Egg Cookbook!

After all, they'rc not called our "golden years" for nothing. They are an ideal summation of the years of work, career, family, change, and progress to what we believe will be our reward at the end of all that work. However, the concept of a life of ease in our senior years is a bit of a modern idea. The fact is, only in the last half of the century has retirement been treated as an entitlement. Generations before worked from the day they could hold a hammer or shovel to the day they could no longer walk. Given our current economic condition, corporate layoffs, the expansion of competition in a global market, and increasing life expectancies, we may very well be going back to those same conditions. The ideal of a life of leisure is changing.

What happened? Well, we could blame the economy, bad leadership, liberal credit, global warming, spacemen, how the planets are aligned, and the list goes on. The real issue for most of us, however, is that we are finally realizing that the average person simply doesn't save enough for a life of leisure or, worse, does save only to lose it again to bad investment decisions and strategies. Enron, MCI, Inc., Global Crossing Limited, Madoff, company-only 401(k) s, Fannie Mae . . . the names reflect some of the worst investment decisions to date, that have cost people billions of hard-earned dollars.

> The most important message that the science of happiness tells us about money is that almost nobody thinks they have enough. In the dark recesses of our brains, free-floating fear tells us that we need more, more, more—or our very survival will be threatened.
>
> In an important Roper Survey, people were asked, on which of 13 basic elements of their lives that they were most satisfied with. They expressed the least satisfaction with the amount of money they had.
>
> Virtually no one feels rich. In a Gallup Poll, the respondents, on average, said that 21 percent of all Americans were rich. But only one-half of 1 percent said that they themselves were rich. People making $10,000 a year believed that those who made $50,000 were rich, and those who made $50,000 thought that people making $200,000 were rich. Those making $200,000 were still scared of their burgeoning bills and feeling the heat of perceived scarcity.
>
> Face facts: Scarcity is burned into your brain. You'll probably never feel as if you have enough money. It's time for you to accept this. And rise above it.

Unfortunately, though, the growing trend in our society is to deny that the feeling of scarcity is an immutable constant, an ingrained fear that should be handed over to the intellect and spirit. Most people, instead, are hell-bent upon trying to soothe their feelings of scarcity by just amassing more money. For example, in a survey of college students, the percentage of those who yearned for financial success above all else almost doubled from 1970 to 1990, reaching 74 percent. Over the same period of time, the percentage of those who primarily aspired to have a meaningful life decreased from 76 percent to 43 percent.

Americans, in particular, are obsessed with money. In a recent large survey, 89 percent of the Americans who were polled said that the United States is "Far too materialistic." But approximately the same percentage said that they wanted even more for themselves.

To that end, Americans are working harder than ever—almost 1 full week per year longer now, than during the 1990s. Until the mid-1990s, Japanese workers averaged the longest hours than anyone else in the world, but now Americans work an average of 31/2 weeks per year more than the Japanese. We also work 6 ½ weeks more than the British, and 12 weeks more than German workers.

This rampant, metastasizing materialism is not making our society happier. It's making us miserable. Virtually every one of the recent studies on money and happiness indicates that money makes people significantly happier only when it relieves abject poverty. Beyond that, money just doesn't do much for happiness. It doesn't matter whether you spend your money at Tiffany or Target—no amount makes a significant difference.

When people yearn for money, though, they don't realize that they're being driven by innate sense of scarcity. They

> think they're being practical—productivewise. They think money will bring five important elements to their lives that will make them happy.
>
> For Sale: Things That People Think Will Bring Happiness
>
> 1. A life of leisure
> 2. Status
> 3. Possessions
> 4. Financial security
> 5. Worldly power
>
> These elements, people think, will make them feel as if they have enough and are good enough. This is a reasonable assumption, one that people have been making for thousands of years.
>
> But it's just not true. Happy people know this. And science proves it.[1]

So what is the recipe for happiness and financial success? Well, the solution starts with us. First, we need to know exactly what we want. "What do you mean?" some ask, "I want to be happy, who doesn't? Isn't that enough?" Unfortunately, no, it's not. The quote from Dan Baker. P. H. D's book, *What Happy People Know*, above shows that what we think will make us happy, doesn't. We need to know how we will be happy and how we will get there because the awful truth is, no one will do the work for us.

Imagine calling your favorite restaurant and asking, "How much does it cost to eat there?" Your question and the answer are simple. Like many things in life, simple and easy are not the same. First you will need to answer some questions, when are you coming in? Are you coming for breakfast, lunch, or dinner? What type of meal do you want? Will you want appetizers? Will you be having drinks? Will you stay for dessert? How many people will be in your party? Once these are answered, the restaurant can then still only give you an estimate of the cost. However, the estimate will be much closer than at the beginning of the conversation, because they would have helped you define what it is that you wanted, your "intellectual framework". Now what happens if I was so busy the day I went in to the restaurant that I had not eaten all day? In fact, I was busy because I had a great day and wanted to celebrate, so I called a few friends and told them dinner was on me! First thing I would do is order drinks and appetizers for everyone because everything on the menu looks good and I am famished. By the time the revelry is done and the check arrives, the cost exceeds the original quote, substantially! This is the "emotions corroding the framework." The plan changed because the emotions changed. A combination of being hungry and adding friends to the list changed the outcome of the original estimate. If I had stuck with the original plan, the outcome and estimate would have been much closer. So what is your plan?

I realize that in the last few decades we had the luxury of defined pensions and a solid Social Security net. Defined pensions were what your father and grandfather received from their company. They put in thirty-five years of service, received a gold watch and a big send off, and then received monthly checks in the mail. Between a defined pension plan, usually a military pension in many cases, from prior service and Social Security, many folks lived very comfortably. It created a sense of well-to-do, and engendered in their children, the baby boomers, that life was always going to be good, and when life is good it is easy to be noble. However, since that time, defined pensions have all but disappeared (the last bastion of government jobs are now losing theirs to 401(k) plans), and Social Security is trimmed back to almost minimal living support. A case can be made that it will be changing dramatically in the coming years. In addition, very few baby boomers and later generations have much, in the way of military service, and consequently no military pension either. Combine this with little savings, throw in a cup of looming inflation, several cups of health care costs, and you have a recipe for disaster. So where do we start on the aforementioned intellectual framework? How can we attain happiness and avoid the recipe for disaster?

PART 1
PLANNING FOR THE FUTURE

Noble Purpose

Don't Survive, Thrive!

David Crowley, a corporate consultant and trainer, developed a curriculum for companies called Own Your Corner. His catchphrase was, "Create an environment where ordinary people casually perform the impossible." With his permission, I have co-opted his idea that I believe to be the cornerstone principle of his excellent work and that is the idea of the "Noble Purpose." In the business world, almost every leadership consultant will tell you that an organization must have a vision/mission statement. However, visions and missions usually don't go far enough. The "noble purpose" gets deeper and includes a more meaningful statement about the nature of an individual's road map. Some have called it a guiding light, but any way you look at it, a noble purpose has power. Without it there can be no synergy between all the elements involved in accomplishing a goal. This becomes your personal constitution or recipe, which keeps you honest and focused.

There are a few basic rules that David Crowley outlines. The first is that it must be short and sweet or more specifically, eleven words or less. Rule number two is that it has to be *captivating* and others-oriented. This is the most difficult because in order to infuse meaning into your retirement years you will have to focus outside of yourself. This is the key ingredient to becoming truly happy. For example, "Not being a burden to my children," is noble and others-oriented, but *not* captivating. The third rule is that it can't be a slogan or trite, like the above example. I will add a fourth to David Crowley's rules, for the individual, which is, it *has* to be positive. The example I used may be noble, but the reason it is not captivating is that it is negative in its tone.

> Example: Use my resources to help friends and family accomplish their goals.

Note that resources can include time or money. Time is far more precious a commodity to many than money. For example, babysitting your grandkids helps your adult kids better accomplish their goals. It will help them spend time together, which will strengthen their marriage. It will allow them to rest. This will allow them to be more focused and effective at their work. So in this example your "resource" was giving up your time so that your adult children can better accomplish their goals. That is not only helping them, but it is allowing you to influence the next generation as well.

Your noble purpose can be as simple as, *Feed hungry people.* That small sentence is packed with ideas and meaning and can inform how you invest your retirement years. The "intellectual framework" Mr. Buffet suggests, and that we will be discussing in the coming pages, should be infused with your noble purpose.

Don't let the bad news of the day (there is always plenty to go around) let you lose your focus.

To discover *your* noble purpose, here are a few questions to guide you:

- What do you want your retirement to look like?
- Why do you want it to look this way?
- What are you willing to give up or change today to reach this target?
- Who or what will help you reach this target?
- How will you expect and plan for the unexpected?

Your answers to these are the raw ingredients for your noble purpose. Look them over once again to determine whether they go deep enough into the true concerns you have for your future.

Don't worry about conciseness as you craft your noble purposes. Your goal is to reach deep inside for a real meaning. You will recognize a noble purpose when you feel it. A true noble purpose stands out. It makes you proud and energizes you.

Also, understand that a good noble purpose can take days to months to develop, depending on the complexity of your situation and how clear your original purpose is.

A noble purpose is hard to create, but simple to read. You will know it when you have "it." It will just fit.

Define Your Goals

Unlike a noble purpose, goals are specific targets we set for ourselves. A noble purpose can have twenty different goals, or maybe just one big one. But ultimately the noble purpose is the driving reason for everything in between.

A goal or objective consists of a projected state of affairs, which a person or a system plans or intends to achieve or bring about—a personal or organizational desired end point in some sort of assumed development. There is also a sense of time involved as well. Many people endeavor to reach goals within a finite time by setting deadlines.

On a personal level, the process of setting goals allows people to specify and then work toward their own objectives—most commonly financial or career-based goals. Goal setting comprises a major component of personal development. In order to achieve a goal, usually one must be focused. When you achieve your goal, it is immensely satisfying.

One acronym, that makes the goal setting process easy to define, is SMAC:

- **Specific**—Need $5,000 a month to free up my time to accomplish my noble purpose, instead of "I want to be comfortable or happy."
- **Measurable**—$5,000 a month adjusted for inflation means, my assets have to grow by 6 percent a year if it does not do this, then, I will have to reduce the amount of time I am dedicating to my noble purpose.
- **Achievable**—20 percent a year returns every year is highly improbable, so, don't build that into your goals.

- **Consistent**—Are your goals consistent with your noble purpose.

To be most effective, goals should be tangible, specific, realistic, and have a time target for completion. For example, setting a goal to go to Mars on a shoestring budget is not a realistic goal while setting a goal to go to Hawaii as a backpacker is a possible goal with possible, realistic plans.

Goal setting also requires motivation. You need to understand why you want the goal. In the motivation film *The Opus*, released in 2008, achievement expert Douglas Vermeeren explains this clearly:

> *When people talk of clarity it often gets described as just writing down your goals. The most important element is often left out. That is finding your motivation. If you want to get to your goals quickly, you have got to get clarity on why you want it. What does it mean to you? Why do you need it in your life? And the stronger and more important, the why—the more power you will have, to pursue that goal.*

In the same film, Dr. Brandon Leach, a professor of psychology at Northwestern University, cites that even if someone is largely self-motivated, he still must have the necessary skill set to reach the goal he has set:

> In my mind, it is completely preposterous to say that motivation is always the most important intangible to possess if one wants to reach a goal of theirs. It's absurd. For example, if some young child sets to be a wizard or witch and is incredibly motivated to do, it's pretty obvious to conclude that he's going to need more than this, oh so important, motivation and seven volumes of Harry Potter.

I would further add that beyond motivation and skill, some people are just not big enough to be NFL linebackers.

Short-term goals expect accomplishment in a short period of time, such as trying to get a bill paid in the next few days. A long-term goal is the opposite—it involves a series of activity and action over an extended period of time. This usually involves many challenges and sacrifices required to be done in aggregate to build to an ultimate reward or target.

For our investment and retirement purposes, long-term goal-planning is the most appropriate. And it needs to be able to answer the following questions when put to test:

- When can you retire?
- Will your money last throughout retirement?
- If you pass away, will your spouse have enough income?
- Will a Down Market ruin your Income Plan?
- What will *taxes* do to your assets?
- What will inflation do to your assets?
- What rate of return *must* you have to survive?
- How do you pay the least amount of taxes now and in the future?

As we mentioned earlier, achieving complex and difficult goals require:

- Focus (noble purpose)
- Long-term diligence and discipline
- Effort

Success requires forgoing excuses and justifications for poor performance or lack of adequate planning; in short, financial success requires emotional maturity and the discipline to stick to the plan. (Remember this point for later in this book!) The measures of belief that people have in their ability to achieve a personal goal also affects that achievement.

Also, remember, how we defined long-term goals are built in the aggregate? Long-term achievements rely on short-term achievements, and many of them. That means, going through a lot of ups and downs in the time it takes to get the job done. Emotional control over small moments of a single day makes a big difference in the long term.

Finally, you can't reach the horizon. Dan Sullivan explains in his book, *Learning to Avoid the Gap: The skill of building lifetime happiness*, that the horizon does not really exist. There is no place where the sky meets the earth. It is a mental construct in the world of setting goals; the horizon is replaced with the ideal. The gap occurs between what the ideal is and where we are. Since we can travel all we want and never reach the horizon, we have to recognize that the ideal is a mental construct as well and cannot be reached. This should not keep us from chasing after the ideal, however. We need to stop and reflect on where we started, how far we have come, before recasting our eyes on the new ideal. If we do not see our progress, we will get discouraged by the fact that we have not reached the ideal. If we do see our progress, it is easier to recast our ideal and press on toward the horizon.

Real Planning

Most retirement planning is sales or product driven. Real planning is purpose or objective driven.

Financial Planning

Personal financial planning is broadly defined as a process of determining an individual's financial goals, purposes in life, and life's priorities after considering his resources, risk profile, and current lifestyle, to detail a balanced and realistic plan to meet those goals. Got all that?

Your goals are used as guideposts to map a course of action on *what needs to be done* to reach those goals. Alongside the data gathering exercise, the purpose of each goal is determined to ensure that the goal is meaningful in the context of your situation. Through a process of careful analysis, these goals are subjected to a reality check by considering your current and future resources available to achieve them. In the process, the constraints and obstacles to these goals are noted. This information will be used later to determine if there are sufficient resources available to get to these goals, and what other things need to be considered in the process. If the resources are insufficient or absent to meet any of the goals, the particular goal will be adjusted to a more realistic level or will be replaced with a new goal. Do you have a headache yet or did you just fall asleep?

Planning often requires consideration of self-constraints in postponing some enjoyment today for the sake of the future, also known as delayed gratification. To be effective, the plan should consider your current lifestyle so that the "pain" in postponing current pleasures is bearable over the term of the plan. In times where current sacrifices are involved, the plan should help ensure that the pursuit of the goal will continue. A plan should consider the importance of each goal and should prioritize each goal. Many financial plans fail because these practical points are not sufficiently considered.

Your financial planning should cover all areas of your financial needs and should result in the achievement of your noble purpose. The scope of planning would usually include the following:

- Picking the right insurance policies for you and your family
- Figuring out when you're going to need cash and how much as well as make sure that it is available at the appropriate time
- Picking the right place to save and invest your money
- Investing with future income stream as a goal
- Retirement and planning to provide a standard of living in your senior years
- Tax planning and avoiding paying on taxes when you don't need to
- Determining how to leave your assets after your death or plan on bouncing the check to the undertaker
- Learning how to teach your children how to manage their finances now and in their future

Financial planning today is big business. Americans have invested trillions of dollars in retirement plans, turning them into the biggest, most valuable asset they own—often worth more than even their homes. As a result, savings protection has become the name of the retirement plan game.[2]

However, good financial planning is more than just a budget and a plan of how to handle your finances. It is a multifaceted approach to managing your money, your income, your goals, and your future. So given all of the above, you don't necessarily just want to treat it like the Sunday newspaper, read once, and throw away. You need to monitor it and pay attention to it regularly. Life changes and so does your finances.

There are usually two camps of people. One is the financial, math type. The other is the social, conceptual type. There are also hybrids that float between these two groups.

The financial/math type person tracks his dollars down to the penny. He uses money software and is an avid reader of any financial information he can find. He is also typically (when unaided) penny wise and pound foolish, as the saying goes.

The social/conceptual type is a long-term thinker. He wants to know that after twenty or thirty years of working, he will have a retirement and can travel around the world. He looks at life in the big picture and sees the horizon of life in large concepts. He, when left to his own devices, is a risk taker and will often not carry about the "pennies," but will take a great deal of risk with the "pounds." The two types rarely like to think about the business of the other. However, in my experience, these two opposites are usually "married" to each other.

Then there are the hybrids. They're not in any a camp per se; they float between the financial/math world and the social/conceptual world like an erratic butterfly bounced and buffeted by the winds of change and fortune. Life takes them up and they get dreamy; life goes down and they worry about having enough money to pay all the bills. They hang on for dear life on a pendulum that keeps going back and forth between the spectrums above. And the only way for most of them to make sure they get some dreams and still pay their bills on time is to budget their way there. It doesn't happen by chance. Yes, there are lottery winners, but you want to build a plan that is not based on statistical possibilities, but on statistical probabilities. It is statistically possible to mix flour, sugar, and eggs randomly together to make a cake, but it is statistically probable to make a cake if you follow a recipe. So I will continue with the recipe.

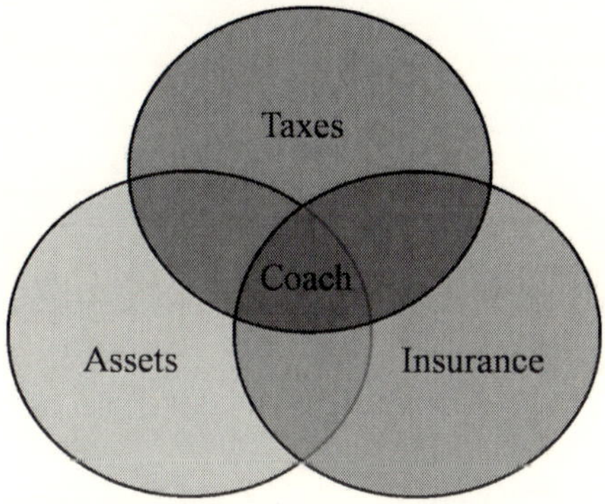

The flour, sugar, and eggs of your "Financial Cake" or in other words the primary building blocks of your plan, consist of Tax Planning (tax avoidance, not tax evasion), Insurance (manage risk at the lowest cost), and Asset Management (includes managing cash flow and hard assets like homes, as well as pooled assets like 401(k)s, IRAs).

A carrot cake does not need chocolate and a chocolate cake does not need carrots, but both of them need flour, sugar, and eggs. Add chocolate to the carrot cake and you will have chocolate carrot cake, but take out the eggs and you don't have anything. When you go to a bakery it would not even cross your mind to ask if they use flour, eggs, and sugar in their cakes. If you have "please seek the advice from a tax advisor before you invest" or something like it on your statement, than you are using a baker that does not put eggs in their cake. You need someone that will either show you how to mix *all* the ingredients of financial and retirement planning together or you need to find someone that can. I will discuss later what model to look for when looking for advice from a professional advisor. You will eliminate a tremendous amount of advisors very quickly by asking them if they know the three primary ingredients of financial cake. Of course, you will probably rephrase the question.

GET IN THE RIGHT MIND-SET

Your mind can be your best friend and your worst enemy. There's an old saying that applies: we can go as far as we're afraid to go. To get to the money you need for a successful life, you need to be able to control your fears and get past them.

Your fears can include things like:

- Not willing to trust and therefore invest in financial vehicles
- Worrying constantly about decisions and second guessing by yourself
- Being afraid to trust others to help with your financial decisions
- Being afraid to dream beyond the immediate financial needs

All of these limitations and others frame and limit the way we think about our money and how we can use it. These limitations also hinder us from moving ahead and pursuing our goals.

This is mental baggage each of us individually needs to face. Avoidance and bottling up fears and concerns only leads to stress, which leads to bad decisions and more fear. Letting go and discussing these limitations with someone trusted, preferably a financial strategist and coach, allows us to bounce our thoughts and ideas off someone else, get their opinion outside of our "box." That advice can help us break through mental walls we've created for ourselves, because they are not held back by them. Only we are.

Just making money in and of itself doesn't give a person peace of mind. We may think it does at first, as we relate more money with the purchase of things we want. That only results in immediate, temporary satisfaction. Eventually we would be bored if there isn't a deeper, more important reason to do it in the first place. That's where your noble purpose comes in. Reaching your goals and living out your noble purpose gives you a true peace of mind. It validates all your efforts and rewards you for trying in the first place. Take the example of Betty and Irene:

> Betty had over five million dollars in solid investment assets. But she insisted on living on an annual budget of only $50,000. Why?
>
> Because she was constantly worried that she would lose her money. She imagined every possible type of financial tragedy—the market would crash, interest rates would drop . . . She worried constantly that she would not have enough money to live on. Did she have peace of mind? You probably can guess the answer to that question.

> Now, Irene had considerably less money than Betty, about $1 million dollars. Irene didn't worry about financial tragedies. Instead, she talked about setting up a trust for her grandchildren, of taking vacations, and about donating money to philanthropic causes. Her mind-set was one of optimism, not tragedy like Betty's.

It's apparent that Irene had peace of mind even though she had far less money than Betty.

This story clearly demonstrated that the amount of money someone has is not the critical determinant of peace of mind about money. Although this particular story is fictitious, I see "Betty's" and "Irene's" quite frequently, and the details may be different, but the mind-sets are identical. Money truly does not buy happiness or peace of mind.

There are strategies that should help create peace of mind for you with regard to finances and your future: [3]

- Raise your awareness
- Understand how the investor's and your mind works
- Don't make emotional decisions

First is the definition of "awareness." We need to know what we are doing and *why.*

Here are some examples of not being aware: You're driving along, talking on your cell phone, on a route that you have driven many times previously. Before you know it you have passed your exit and/or arrived at your destination without any recollection of how you got there. In these situations, you had a lapse of consciousness. You were on auto-pilot, without awareness of what you were doing.

Many people act unconsciously when they invest their money. They do it the way their parents did or continually follow advice that sounds good in the moment, but isn't part of any clear plan.

Another type of unconsciousness relates to thoughts. Thousands of thoughts run through our brains constantly, at a very fast rate. A term for these random thoughts is "mind chatter." Your mind is most likely chattering while people are talking to you. Your mind is chattering as you read this now and as I write this. Many experts in the field of psychology say that our inner thoughts become so programmed over a period of time that they become unconscious. Unless we make an effort to recognize our mind chatter and then reprogram or change it, it keeps telling us the same thoughts over and over. And, what's worse is that we tend to follow those thoughts as instructions unconsciously. It's almost like we are brainwashed. The following is an example of Mind Chatter:

> Remember, Betty? Her mind chatter was filled with negative and unpleasant thoughts . . . thoughts about financial disaster, constantly worried about preserving her $5,000,000. Her thoughts about money centered on disaster, on catastrophic events that would destroy her financial security. On the other hand, Irene's mind-chatter centered on positive ideas about how she would utilize her money, to enjoy life.

What can you do if unconscious mind chatter is destroying your peacc of mind? The answer is simple.

Become conscious of negative chatter and change it to positive mind-chatter.

You've probably heard of the book, *The Secret*. It's labeled in a mysterious looking book cover; it has big hype about a universal, mystical secret that if discovered leads to riches and success. It was a bestseller for months as a result. You know what the solution to *The Secret* really is? Think positive! The book goes into a lot more spins and anecdotes, but the core principle is exactly that: think positive. Expect good things, look for good things, wish for good things, act as if good things are going to happen, and you know what? You've just boosted your awareness to take advantage of good opportunities when they come along.

Negative thoughts are reflected in how we feel and behave. In an audio recording called *The Lost Art of Happiness* by philosopher J. P. Moreland, he discusses a study (I am quoting from memory so it won't be exact) that said, what we are thinking about before we go to bed will shape our day. What do most people do before going to bed? They watch the news. No wonder in the wealthiest country in the history of mankind most people are miserable. We watch an hour of *bad* news and then wake up thinking that civilization is coming to an end. Perhaps one of the single greatest things that you can do to improve your outlook on life is to stop watching the news!

When you are feeling or behaving negatively, ask yourself, "What thought is causing me to feel and behave this way?" Teach yourself to make unconscious thoughts conscious.

More Mind Chatter Examples:

> For example, if Betty had forced herself to become more aware of her negative thoughts, she would have consciously realized how destructive they were. Knowing that, she could have said, "Betty, stop thinking that way. It makes you feel terrible. You need to focus on positive thoughts, 'I'm not a prophet, and how would I know that the stock market is going to crash?' Or, "I have a competent financial advisor. I have developed an intellectual framework and market fluctuations no matter how dramatic are built into the plan. Stop this catastrophic thinking."

Bringing her unconscious thoughts to a conscious level, and challenging the negative thoughts, she will have more peace of mind about her financial future.

In summary, there are four ways to raise your level of consciousness:

1. Become more aware of self and environment
2. Recognize and challenge negative mind-chatter
3. Replace negative thoughts with positive ones

4. Get the facts! (If you know the right things, you don't need to know everything.)

Now that we are thinking more positively about life in general, let's move to the investor's mind. Everyone who has money in an investment is an investor and their mind dictates the good and bad investment decisions they make. There are three parts of the investor's mind:

1. **The cognitive part**—that is what you know, your knowledge. This can be facts, concepts, statistics, and so forth. Logic rules here.
2. **The instinctual part**—this controls your inborn patterns of behavior—like people instinctually want to survive, to avoid pain, to be nourished with food, to feel good about themselves, and to experience pleasure. These instincts are at an unconscious level. They function without our permission. We're born with them.
3. **The emotional part**—your feelings. Examples of feelings are glad, sad, mad, anxious, afraid, etc. Most people don't realize the power of emotions. Dale Carnegie said, "People aren't creatures of logic. They are creatures of emotion." And when push comes to shove, and emotions and logic collide, emotions are the winner. We like to think that, as human beings, we behave rationally, that our decisions are always made with our rational or cognitive mind. Not so!!!

So let's take the following three simple rules of investing and build a simple formula: C = Cognitive, I = Instinctual, and E = Emotional:

1. Owning (stocks) is better than loaning (bonds, CDs).
2. Diversify your portfolio to reduce risk. (Don't put all your money in just a few stocks, or in one category of asset or even in one country, more on this later.)
3. Buy low. Sell high!

If most people cognitively know these three rules, then why do so many investors fail to follow them?

C < I + E

Here is an example from the dietary world. The following statement will save you thousands of dollars over your lifetime. It is the secret to losing weight. Ready!?

MOVE MORE, CONSUME LESS.

Like I said in the opening pages, life is simple, but it is not easy.

So if it is simple, why do dieters fail? What's wrong in both examples (the rules of investing and staying fit) is that the instinctual and emotional parts of our minds override the cognitive part.

I + E > C

So how do we unconsciously sabotage ourselves?

We consume fattening, but great-tasting food and the financial equivalent is the media hype on investing? We read "Get rich quick" (greed) articles and the "doom and gloom" (fear) rhetoric? The media hype on money topics is typically geared to activate our instinctual urges such as pleasure and survival and our emotions such as panic, urgency, excitement, and fear. Jane Bryant Quinn, a well-known financial expert, refers to it as "investment pornography." I call it investment junk food. Just because something is in your mouth and you are chewing and swallowing, does not mean it is good for you. It does not mean it is actually food, either. (What exactly is a cheese puff?) If we're not conscious enough to activate our cognitive mind, our instincts and emotions sure can get us into trouble (like eating a whole bag of cheese puffs in a single sitting), and lead us away from prudent investing (and eating). These messages destroy our peace of mind and result in unnecessary distress. The media is public enemy #1 to peace of mind. Remember what their business is, entertainment, to sell advertising and in some cases, books.

> The Cognitive Mind is overpowered by (Instinct + Emotion) x Media

When we factor the media messages into the *conscious investor formula*, then the cognitive part of our mind doesn't stand a chance. It's no wonder peace of mind is such an elusive state for the typical investor today.

MOTIVATION

The other mental block many of us tend to have that affects our financial decisions is our motivations. Motivation is the "why" in what we do, when we do it, and how we do it.

When we get into the why of spending we get into motives. A motive is:[4]

- Something that causes a person to act in a certain way, do a certain thing, etc.; incentive
- The goal or object of a person's actions: *i.e., her motive was revenge*

Causation and reasons can range from primal desires to logical conclusions that something should be bought with the money we have (or borrow). The best place to start with the what and why of spending is the psychology behind it. A Maslow's view of the world basically takes a pyramid and states that the human mind is unable to dwell on aesthetic issues if it has not yet satisfied its basic needs. See below:

Maslow's Need Hierarchy Model [5]

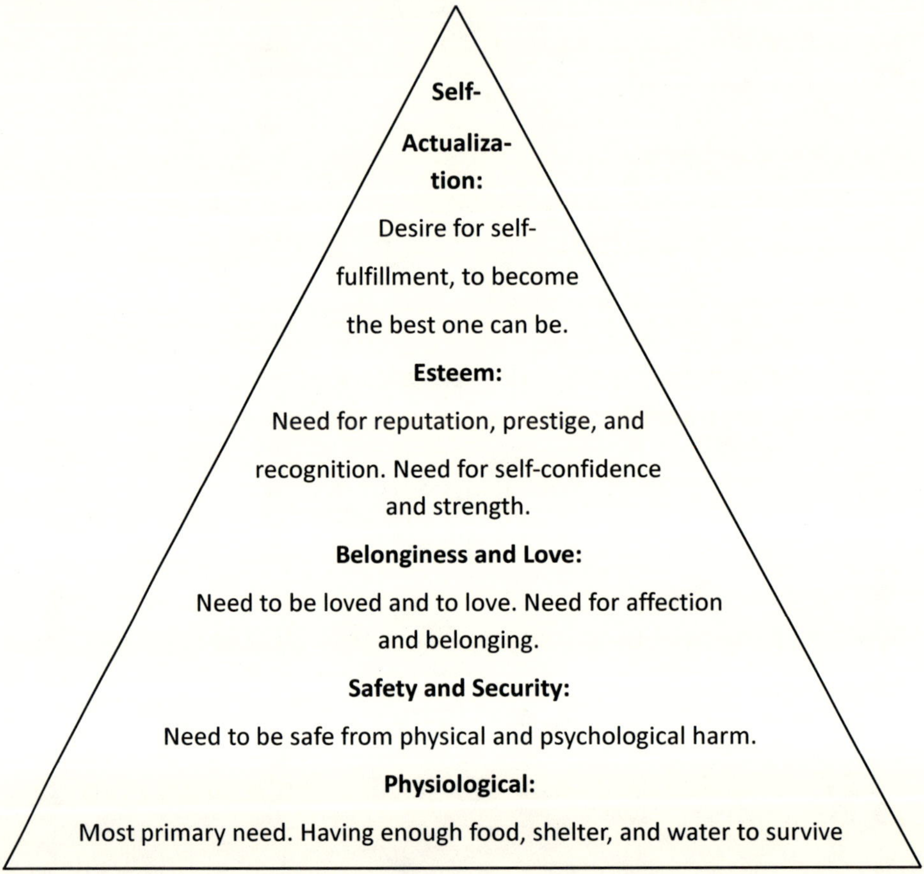

At the bottom of the pyramid are things like feeding hunger, seeking shelter, and securing resources to survive. As these basic needs are met, then psychologically the mind is freed up to think on higher levels and takes on loftier issues higher up the pyramid. However, if the basic needs begin to be left behind again, the human mind drops back down the pyramid to start again.

Just as much as you put importance on what you want and when, you should also be able to identify why you want something. Marketers look for three key ingredients of customer behavior when applying their marketing campaign:[6]

- Motive measures why people want what they want (the belief that a product or service is good)
- Opportunity measures access to what they want (can they find it?)
- Means measures the ability to obtain what they want (can they afford it?)

Some of the more obvious components of any motive are:[7]

- Your situation, context, or problem, in which you find yourself.
- Your role in that situation (solo choice, shared choice, etc).
- Your goal in that situation (i.e., your motive, what you want).
- Your goal criteria—the desired features and benefits related to the goal.
- Your perceived choices in the situation (brand A, brand B, brand C, . . .)
- Your anticipated outcome (obtaining what I want)

If you know the parts of the "Why" you spend, you will understand your spending habits even better. We are emotional beings, and we buy emotionally too. We are driven to buy through one (or a combination) of the following motives:

- Make a gain
- Receive social approval
- Receive pleasure
- Avoid pain
- Boost pride
- Fear of loss

As a result of the above, if we identify why we spend the way we do, we have a start. Just knowing why is not enough. If we really want to control our spending, we then need to make judgments, prioritize, be disciplined, and control our spending. Once again our diet is a great analogy. We can make a judgment on whether we should eat a bunch of donuts. Maybe, I should eat breakfast first (prioritize). Maybe I should eat half a donut (discipline) or maybe I should not eat any donuts now or the rest of the day (control).

We need to make judgments about our desires and motives. Are they important? Are they necessary? Are they silly? Are they entertaining? We individually are the only ones who can truly determine how our motives land in each of these categories.

Once identified, we need to prioritize our motives. Yes we can have silly reasons, but there's nothing wrong with that. However, they should take a second seat to our critical motives such as food, shelter, warmth, etc. They should also be behind secondary critical motives such as what we need to maintain our source of income (our jobs), and what we need to move ahead and improve our situation.

We need to keep discipline with our spending motives, and control them instead of the spending controlling us.

What You Really Need to Maintain Your Lifestyle

A retirement plan is dependent on a few moving parts:

- How much money you saved up to the point of actually retiring
- How much time you have to save prior to your actual retirement date
- The projected rates of return you are able to earn
- What kind of lifestyle you plan on having

In a personal or family budget, all sources of income (inflows) are identified, and expenses (outflows) are planned with the intent of matching outflows to inflows (making ends meet.) However, for retirement, you have to think in terms of distributing (distribution planning) your wealth so that it pays for your retirement. Your strategy should ideally produce enough money to cover your life expectancy time period, an emergency cash fund, and a buffer to protect your overall account from the continuing effects of inflation. And inflation is the most overlooked and underfigured part of a person's plan.

So the first step is to figure out what your current cash flow is. This would include money coming in consistently from Social Security, pensions, rental income, or anything else that is consistent. This will be your base pay.

Secondly, assess your current account values and assets. The assets should be income-producing, so your automobiles and home do not count. We are not trying to figure out your net worth, your net worth will always be separatc from income planning and cash flow planning. This means quantifying via total Market Value your investment portfolios. The process includes all your company 401(k) s, personal IRAs, bonds, government securities, etc. Once again, keep property assets out of the picture (i.e., the house, boat, jewelry, etc.) If you're not planning on selling it, we can't use it for cash flow.

Thirdly, determine a realistic estimate of how long you will live. The math formula involved essentially uses single life expectancy tables to determine expectancy. If you have a spouse or dependents, then you would use the related table for that scenario. Life expectancy tables are available online at:

www.irs.ustreas.gov/ Search for publication 590 or use the current average of 82.4.

Keep in mind, the one flaw with these charts is that they are based on actual, historical mortality rates. Those are death statistic figures that come from the past. And with modern medicine and hygiene, people are living longer than previous generations. Further, the same statistics will change again as numbers come in from the 2010 Census. So add to your result five to ten years to be on the safe side.

Finally, calculate against a range of reasonable interest rates (I start with 5 percent). The result should be what you can expect your retirement total to provide you annually. You multiply this by your life expectancy and you have the income figure you need to live on financially for your retirement. This is your target. If the number is too small to live on for the entire period, then you don't have enough to start with.

If you don't have enough to live on, there are only four solutions

- Work longer
- Save more
- Get better returns
- Spend less

Generally the best solutions are a combination. I am real comfortable saying someone can succeed in retirement if the numbers all work with 5 percent returns. U.S. Treasuries have averaged just over 6 percent for the last thirty-six years. I realize that right now we are seeing historically low rates, but if you follow the simple principles outlined in the following pages, you will see that you can put science, history, and math on your side if, of course, you can keep your emotions out of the way.

All that I have outlined to determine if you have enough to live on can be done by any competent financial advisor. If you are working with someone that has *any* of your assets and they have not done the relatively easy plan outlined above, then you are working with a sales person, not an advisor, strategist, or coach.

Here are a few pitfalls, you should avoid in the planning process, once again any decent strategist and/or coach should be able to help you with this:[8] [9]

- **Having unrealistic expectations**—this is probably the most common error people make when they're planning their retirement. If your grocery costs are $600 a month, then it isn't reasonable to only budget $300 in an effort to save money. So keep all of your expectations, even the good ones for saving money, realistic and fair when you plan your retirement need. Solution: Reduce the amount you spend on these items rather than trying to totally eliminate these small luxuries. A good financial advisor can spot these problems and figure this all out very easily, saving you time and headaches.
- **Not Having a Written Plan**—it's often said that if you fail to plan, then you plan to fail. A written retirement plan will not only help you keep on track, but also help you to evaluate where and when your budget needs to be revised. Yes, it may seem formal and unnecessary, but you will thank your stars later when you need to refer back to your roadmap how to make distribution decisions.
- **Mistaking luxuries for necessities**—you're absolutely convinced that those weekly massages are lifesaving. But you could probably live without them; if you had to, right? Many things we spend money on dressing up as needs when they're really wants, so don't let yourself be fooled. If you don't have to have it and you don't have a comfortable place for it in your budget, then it's time to let it go, at least for a while.
- **Expecting windfalls**—That hot stock you bought may earn back double what you paid for it in six months, and it may not. This is as silly as expecting a 10 percent return just because it was the S&P average for last year. That twelve-month CD will come due next month, but your car may break down and need major repairs. So to keep your bottom line healthy and keep your sanity at the same time, don't add the income from these sorts of "windfalls" into your

budget. You'll still find a place for that money, if and when it comes.

- **Buying before trying—**Rather than budgeting for that new motorcycle you think you need to help you save on your gas bill, how about renting one first—in January, in the winter? Do you still think it's such a great idea? Many times we jump into things we're stuck making payments on forever, all with the best of intentions. Trying some of these things out first could save us a great deal of money we could spread out in other places in our budgets. So the next time you have a bright idea, try it out before you plunk down your money—and you won't have to cringe every time you make out that payment check.
- **Forgotten Items—**Gifts for birthdays, graduations, weddings, and showers are some of the big items which don't make the budgeting list, but which will also throw a budget into chaos. Other forgotten items include car insurance, professional association, or club dues, subscriptions, Internet fees, and other kinds of expenses, which show up only periodically or annually. Solution: Set a price range for gift purchases rather than shopping impulsively. Take annual costs such as dues, subscriptions, fees, and car insurance and divide out by twelve months. Keep a running tally of all annual costs and check periodically as costs go up or down for each item.

Compare Your Goals to Your Current Status

This is the point where things get really interesting. You know where you want to be (your goals), you know what you need to do to get there (your budget and financial plan), now you need to determine how far you need to go in between. This is the comparison of your goals with your current status. Everybody will be different.

Examine your revenues now versus retirement

All planning boils down to managing cash flow. In retirement the cash flow is no longer coming from a paycheck. It comes from a variety of places. Knowing these will help.

Assessment

Most folks assume they will not be working after retirement. That's understandable, after an entire life of working from the age of sixteen until sixty plus, not working sounds really enticing. Of course, along with that assumption is another one: that there will be money from somewhere to continue to pay the cost of living. The majority believe that by the time retirement occurs, there will be enough in Social Security and a retirement account to cover the bills. Traditional retirement accounts (IRAs and 401(k)s) have always been touted as the best saving vehicle for your retirement. The promise of tax-deferred savings makes your savings grow quickly. However, there's a trade-off. We have been told that you're supposed to pay less in taxes when you're retired than you will when you are working. Well, you know what they say about assuming? So most people are building into their plan that taxes are not going up and that they will need less money to live on in retirement than when they are working? In my experience, governments raise taxes and people don't change their lifestyle after retiring. If anything, the extra free time needs to be filled with activities that cost money.

Typical revenues for most people are their regular paycheck income and the assumption of Social Security. If you've been employed for the minimum number of years, each year you receive an annual statement from the Social Security Administration detailing how much you can expect to receive monthly when you're eligible to receive benefits. They even break out the difference taking the benefits at 62 versus 67 and 70 (which can be considerable).

For example, take the benefits of a thirty-eight-year old that has worked and paid into Social Security for twenty-two years. If he stopped working and then waited until his retirement dates, he would get the following benefits:

- Applies at age sixty-two, receives $1,620 a month
- Applies at age sixty-seven, receives $2,354 a month
- Applies at age seventy, receives $2,924 a month

Now, if you also have retirement accounts, you need to make the decision as to whether you are going to use those funds right away or keep them in the accounts, earning more. Some accounts require distributions. For instance, a 457 account requires distribution upon separation, regardless of retirement or not. A 401(k) can stay put or be rolled over to a traditional IRA, but by age seventy-and-a-half you need to start taking minimum withdrawals or required minimum distribuitons (RMDs). The penalties are severe for not distributing when required. Your planning will need to take into account these dates and distribute accordingly.

Maybe you're not ready to fully retire just yet. Part-time work may suit you just fine. That, with a pension could be more than enough to put off a Social Security benefit and avoids retirement account dates because you are still working. Either way, your revenue picture has to take into account all these variables to know what you're going to have to spend each month.

BOOST YOUR INCOME

Maybe you've come to the realization, however, that despite having all of the above, your current retirement revenue is just not going to be enough for how you want to live in retirement. Many folks put off this test until they actually get to retirement. Then, instead of taking the cruise they wanted and planned for, they're stuck spending their days watching TV in an apartment because that's all they can afford.

Assuming taxes will be lower and that you will live on less is wishful thinking. If you live on $50K, save $5K a year in your 401(k) and are paying $10K toward principle and interest on a mortgage, then you are effectively living on $35KI have heard multiple times that the rule of thumb is that you live on 80 percent of what you lived on before you retired. The reality is that you live on the same amount when you retire ($35k in this example) and the first few years of retirement it may go up due to traveling, playing more golf, etc. What you need to consider, is that you will be living (not surviving). In other words, the very nature of having extra time costs money. While working, you are making money and at the same time not spending it. When retired, you're not making money and you are spending it.

If you can't reduce expenses comfortably, then the alternate option is to generate more income. Take on a second job, work nights, or on the weekends. Provide independent services from your years of experience where you control your work hours. Start your own business based on a hobby or skill. The Internet has broken all the barriers and obstacles that bar many from opening a business under the old brick and mortar approach. Today, you can have a business selling items on e-Bay or other auction Web sites, providing written and verbal services through other companies, filling out surveys, or being a consultant. The type of business you do is only limited by what you think you can do, and how much time you can devote to the effort.

Let's say you're already retired and find that extra income is needed. You're in a wonderful situation, believe it or not. Unlike many other job hunters, you have a funding base already from your existing retirement sources. So you have the ability to take on riskier employment with bigger rewards. Commission-based, project-based, maybe even putting out your own shingle. Many advisors tell new business owners not to quit their day job when first starting out, and your retirement income already is the next best thing. Why? Unlike most businesses, you can ride out weeks and months when things don't work out. You can also underbid on projects because your overhead is lower, just because you don't have to pay yourself a salary.

Don't think that you'll be viable being a senior-aged employee? Think again. The demand for experience is growing exponentially. With so many baby boomers retiring, depth and knowledge are in short supply in many industries. This creates an inherent demand for knowledgeable staff who can hit the ground running with little training in a technical field, or for the flexibility of experienced consultants and advisors.[10]

What are Your True Assets?

You've identified your revenues and now probably figured out a decent idea of whether you're going to have enough to cover your desired cost of living in retirement. What about your assets? The first things that come to mind are:

- Savings accounts (Nonqualified)
- Retirement accounts (Qualified)

- Property (Examples would be farming, timber, rental, home etc.)
- Interests
- Partnership/ownerships/stakeholder claims

Here we include also the non-income-producing assets because we are now looking at your estate. The fact is your estate assets are bigger than you think.

Of course, in 2010, there is an exception of not-applicable federal estate tax, so if you need to pass something very expensive on to heirs, 2010 would be a very good year to die! Just kidding!

The final estate tax number of $3,500,000 today or $1,000,000 as it has been in the past has not been nailed down. This, of course, remains to be seen. Conceptually, what we will be discussing will not change and if I was a betting man, I would bet on a lower number and not a higher one.

"But I don't have anything close to that amount, so I don't need to worry about it."

You might be closer than you think.

Most people grossly underestimate the value of their estate. Estates include accounts, compounding interest, homes, and second homes rising in market value, art and item collections, business partnerships, property, etc—as you name it. Anything owned is part of the estate.

The average home in California today is being purchased for $250,000 to $300,000 (we're not talking about San Francisco). In 1975, the average suburban home went for $40,000. That's a $210,000 to $260,000 difference. Fast-forward another twenty or thirty years, and it's likely to be valued close to $500,000 to $750,000.

Add on the value of other estate items like cars, collections, furniture, items in your house, and you're now increasing by another $100,000. Then take into account savings, CDs, portfolios, property interests, investments, and any other financial tools held in the estate, and you start getting a big number real fast. That's just the average, middle-income family. A successful family that is smart with their money will easily exceed the limits.

The bottom line is your assets are bigger than you think. One million dollars today grows to $2,000,000 in just ten years at a 7 percent return. The IRS takes about half of the assets above the limit in the year the inheritance takes place, from the beneficiary. That means if the beneficiary doesn't have the cash on hand to pay the tax, he or she will have to liquidate something to get it. That usually means selling the family house they just inherited, for example.

Money without purpose is burden defined. The possession of wealth without a clear declarative purpose leads the investor to the wrong conclusion that money is a means unto itself. With this mind-set, the greater the wealth, the heavier the burden of caring, managing, and allocating assets becomes. To fully enjoy wealth, you must have a deeper purpose and value for money. Yes, I am reminding you once again of the need for the noble purpose.

The reality check is *you are already rich!* In comparison to all of humanity that has inhabited this planet in the past and today, you already have vast amounts of wealth available to you. You have access to food, clothing, education, shelter, technology, and freedom unimaginable just a few decades ago. Ethical free market capitalism has made you rich. Enjoy it and make a difference in the lives of others.

Attaining Retirement

As you close in on the retirement date, many think that the rules of the game change. The truth is that retirement is not a different set of rules; it is a whole new game.

Accumulation versus Distribution

If there is a critical section in this book to remember, it is this one.

Until now, the idea of increasing your retirement account for most was probably focused on deposits. That's not surprising. Banks, financial providers, brokers, and the media constantly advertise Roth this, IRA that, savings account here, CD there. More importantly, you had time on your side. But now the goal of retirement has either gotten close enough to now focus your attention on it, or has finally come to pass, and the elements of maximizing the ultimate value of your IRA have changed. Instead of just contributing as much as you can through occasional deposits, you now have realized you need to earn as much as you can and create an ongoing income. In other words, your retirement assets are now changing into an income stream, or better known as your paycheck.

Saving for retirement is, believe it or not, the easy part. In many ways, managing your investments so that you don't run out of money is trickier than saving it in the first place. People don't think about the risk of outliving their money, but they should put as much effort into trying to make wealth last as they did to building that wealth in the first place. Possibly the biggest challenge of your retirement planning is to take the money you've amassed over your life to this point and turn it into a reliable income stream to support a postwork life that could last as long as or maybe even longer than your work life. While amassing a retirement nest egg can make you feel like you completed a long journey, the real trip starts when you begin to figure out how to use or "cook" that nest egg.

Unfortunately, not every investor is going to be able to retire with a portfolio that can provide sufficient income to meet their current and future needs. In addition to Social Security and any pension or retirement income, the average investor will likely need to draw upon principal from their investment portfolio, in addition to using the interest, dividend, and capital gains income it generates, to meet expenses. The factors weighing into whether or not the investor's assets will likely be sufficient are many, and the effects of both inflation and less-than-expected investment returns can dramatically impact the retirement plan (if we learned anything from 2008, that should be it). Various well-known studies indicate that a "safe" withdrawal rate falls in the 3.0 percent to 5.0 percent range. Harvard University did a study to determine how much could be safely withdrawn from their endowment fund without depleting the principal. Assuming a portfolio of 50 percent stocks and 50 percent bonds and cash, Harvard's analysts calculated that 4 percent could be withdrawn the first year and then adjust the subsequent year's withdrawals for inflation. For example, if there was 5 percent inflation, the second year's withdrawal would be 4.2 percent (4 percent × 1.05) on the initial asset value. A 5 percent rate is considered to be at the outer limit of acceptable levels of withdrawals. This would require holding 80 to 100 percent of the portfolio in stocks, a level few retirees would find comfortable, especially given what happened with the market in 2008. These studies were based on historical data, and future results will vary and will definitely impact these estimated "safe withdrawal rates." These are numbers that are much lower than the average investor plans on dealing with when a broker pontificates about S&P 500 returns that have averaged 10 percent for the last X number of years.

To complicate matters, we have to deal with taxes. It's usually the biggest check of your life—your lump-sum distribution from your pension and/or 401(k). There's not a ton of options to choose from. You have three choices on what to do:[11]

- Roll over the money to an IRA
- Stay put in the company plan (for as long as allowed) or rollover to a new employer's plan. (This is almost never a good idea. Real-life examples of when it works are nil to almost none).
- Take a lump-sum distribution and pay the related taxes now

The following factors affect your decision:[12]

- When will you need the money?
- What will your tax bracket be in retirement?
- How is your health?
- How much money will you need for retirement?
- How much is the lump-sum distribution?
- How old are you?
- What is your estate/legacy plan?
- Who will pay the income tax?
- Will you be working again?
- Is creditor protection a big issue for you?
- What are the fees associated with the current and/or future accounts?
- Do you think the tax laws will be changing?
- How old is your spouse/partner?
- How will forced distributions have an effect on your plan?

Remember our discussion about goal-setting and financial planning? It would probably be really helpful right now to have that plan to refer to in answering some of these questions, wouldn't it?

Having been so busy chasing investment returns all their working lives, people probably neglected the distribution part of the equation altogether, and thus risk losing a whopping amount of what they've earned to the taxman.[13] Most haven't yet experienced the shock of losing the bulk of a retirement account to taxes. When this happens, one wishes there was a way to reverse the damage. But by then it's too late.[14]

A lifetime of doing everything right can be shattered by this one catastrophic event. In the 2007-2008 NFL season, the New England Patriots were thirty-five *seconds* shy of the perfect season. The New York Giants had an ugly season, but won the Super Bowl in the last thirty-five seconds. What team would you want your portfolio to emulate?

Do You Really Ever Stop Saving?

According to the Federal Reserve, the savings rate in this country hasn't exceeded 6 percent since 1995; that's down from approximately 12.5 percent in early 1981. This number has jumped recently due to the terror of the 2008 stock market collapse, but I suspect, as things improve, they will drop back to the historical lows. There are plenty of debates about whether the savings rate accurately reflects the actual number of people who are saving. But there's no doubt that the average American isn't saving enough.

Hey, it's a free country. You earned your money. You should spend it however you like! Right? But if you're spending every dime you make throughout your career, don't complain when your 60s roll around and you're still a slave to the alarm clock.

If you feel it is difficult to begin saving, especially on a retirement and limited income, simply start with a small amount. Maybe you begin with $10 a week initially. While this amount won't add up all that quickly, the important thing is to start putting something away and to make it a habit. After a few weeks, you won't even notice that $10 missing so you can bump it up to $15 or $20 after a month or so. Soon, you will begin to get used to that money not being there and can slightly increase it again.

Alternatively, the opposite can occur too. People hoard their savings too much. Individuals nearing or in retirement may be inclined to reduce their investment risk on their savings by placing more emphasis on income and principal stability than on capital appreciation. It's important to realize, however, that relying on conservative investments such as CDs, government bonds, etc., may seem safe, but could actually expose your portfolio to inflation and increase the risk of running out of money in your senior years. Inflation at 3 percent takes out $0.41 of each dollar over thirty years. [15] That's almost half a portfolio. Also CDs are typically taxed higher than an equivalent money market account at a custodian like Schwab Institutional. CDs are the modern-day equivalent of burying your money. That is why they are fondly referred to as certificates of depreciation.

THE EMERGENCY FUND

Learn to save for financial emergencies. Even if you feel robust and invincible, a single emergency room trip or car accident could force you to put large balances on credit cards, causing interest to accrue and more debt to pile up. That rainy day will happen, it's not a matter of "if," it's a matter of "when." If your tire goes flat and you can't pay upfront for the replacement, for instance, you're stuck with charging it or reducing funds earmarked for necessities. That's where the emergency fund fits in.

Financial advisors suggest having enough savings in an easily accessible account to cover your living expenses for six months in the event of illness, job loss, or other serious emergency. The last thing you want to do is being forced to rely on credit cards or a loan, which could simply compound the problem.

The reason you want to have six months of expenses saved up is that the most common reason for the need of an emergency fund is due to a sudden loss of income or "unexpected" expense. If you or your spouse loses a job, you still have bills to pay and it may take a few months to find suitable new employment. It is best to plan for a worst-case scenario so that the smaller "unexpected" emergencies such as replacing the hot water heater that just went out will be easily covered. The reason I put "unexpected" in quotes is because it really should be *expected.* Since the "unexpected" happens consistently and constantly what is unexpected is the *when* not the *If!* There will always be unexpected events. It is not *If* they will happen, it is *when* they will happen. Plan for them!

If you currently don't have an emergency fund or find it difficult to save money, the key is to start small. You have to realize that accumulating one month's worth of expenses will take some time, let alone three to six months. If you set your immediate goals to be small and manageable, you will have a better chance in reaching them.

The best way to get started would probably be through your bank, however, considering the tax implications. Bank products are typically taxed as regular income. Brokerage accounts are typically taxed as a dividend and for most people, this is a lower rate. For many, the difference is pennies, but for some it can be considerable. That said, during the Clinton era, banking interest was cheaper, so the issue may flip-flop. Either way, open up a new account if you currently don't have one and begin to save with this first. The next step is to get into the habit of making regular deposits into this account. Whether it is weekly, bi-weekly, or monthly, create a schedule and stick to it. Once you make saving automatic, you won't even have to think about it.

You should start with a savings account because it is simple to use and generally does not cost anything. The convenience factor is what is important when getting started. As your account grows you will want to find an account that earns reasonable interest so that saving the money works to your benefit. The next best options to look into are money market accounts or short-term certificate of deposits (CDs).

It is important to keep this emergency fund in a place that will be fairly liquid so that you can get to the money quickly in the event of an emergency. You also don't want to have this money tied into stocks or mutual funds because the volatility of the market could cause you to lose money over the short term.

The idea is to have enough money available so you won't have to rack up credit card debt or sell investments in case of a financial emergency, such as a job loss, unexpected medical bills, or even last-minute airfare for a funeral. Your money should be safe and accessible.

Get What is Due to You Wisely (Medicare and Social Security)

The axiom, "Knowledge is power" must have been written with government programs in mind.

Social Security

Social Security establishes the age at which workers and their families may begin receiving retirement benefits from the government. If you were born before 1938, this is set at age sixty-five. If you were born between 1938 and 1954, the full retirement age increases progressively from sixty-five up to sixty-six. If your birth year is 1955 or later, your full retirement age increases progressively up to sixty-seven. Age sixty-seven is currently the oldest full retirement age, though I expect this to go up in the very near future.

You may begin taking Social Security retirement benefits at age sixty-two. But keep in mind, if you begin before reaching your full retirement age (FRA), the monthly benefits are paid at a permanently reduced amount (up to 20 to 25 percent less) to reflect receiving benefits for more years. This is not actually bad, but consider these scenarios:

> **Under Full Retirement Age (FRA) and Have Substantial Earnings**—it is generally not to your advantage to begin receiving reduced Social Security retirement benefits if your job pays enough to maintain your standard of living. Because you have not yet reached your full retirement age, you will lose a significant portion of your monthly benefit due to the earnings offset limits.
>
> **Under FRA and Not Enough Income for Living Expenses**—it may be advisable to begin early, though reduced benefits if your income is not sufficient to meet your living expenses. Your benefits will not be reduced based on your wages if you earn less than the allowed offset limit.
>
> **At FRA**—you may begin getting full benefits at your full retirement age and no earning limits apply. So, after you reach full retirement age, you can enjoy your full Social Security benefits and retirement job income.
>
> **After FRA—**if you do not need your Social Security retirement benefit for living expenses, you may want to delay beginning to get benefits until *after* your full retirement age (up to age seventy). When they begin, monthly benefits will be increased substantially above the base (FRA) amount, increasing at about 7 to 8 percent for each year of delay beyond full retirement age.

If, after retirement, you will be relying on a mix of Social Security and savings from your nest egg (IRA, 401(k) etc.)

for income, reducing the number of pretax dollars you have to spend is startlingly important.

Social Security benefits become taxable for a married couple filing jointly when one-half of their total Social Security benefit added to all their other income is greater than $32,000 or $25,000 for a single individual.

In 2007, a couple getting the average Social Security benefit receives $20,556. Half of that is $10,278. That means they can withdraw about $19,500 from tax-advantaged savings for a total income of $40,000 and pay few, if any, federal taxes at all, in part because Social Security remains tax-free and the couple gets extra standard deductions for being older than sixty-five.

In many parts of the country, that is a comfortable income—particularly for people who own their home free and clear. Add a mortgage to the equation and the picture changes significantly.

If this couple has a monthly $1,000 mortgage payment and opts to pay it by pulling savings out of a 401(k) or other tax-advantaged account, they'll not only pay taxes on Social Security, they'll also be taxed on the money they withdraw from their 401(k). Altogether, they would need to withdraw $39,000 from the account to cover the extra mortgage payments and taxes, which increases their tax bill from nearly zero to about $4,000. We will further explore why paying off your mortgage makes sense later in this book as well.

If this couple, who could otherwise live comfortably on $40,000, happens to withdraw another $6,000 from their 401(k) for a total of $45,000, then their taxable Social Security and income will likely push them into the 25 percent tax bracket, raising what they'll pay in taxes to about $5,700.

Between Social Security and an untaxed nest egg (qualified assets), people are thrown into a position where all of their withdrawals and the majority of their Social Security are taxable. The longer people can defer touching their untaxed nest egg (IRA's and 401(s k)s), the better off they are. Rule of thumb—if you're still working, don't take Social Security yet. If you're not working, take it. The breakeven is twelve to sixteen years out for delaying benefits and may not be worth it, especially if you die sooner.

For People *not* Receiving Social Security Benefits:		
If you're . . .	**You can earn up to this amount with no penalty:**	**If your retirement job pays you more than that amount:**
Any age	No limit	There is **no impact** on your benefits either now or in the future.

For People *who are* Receiving Social Security Benefits:[16]		
If you're . . .	**You can earn up to this amount with no penalty:**	**If your retirement job pays you more than that amount:**
Under full retirement age (sixty-two to sixty-five)	$14,160 in 2009	Your benefits are reduced by $1 for every $2 earned over the limit.
Reaching full retirement age this year (sixty-five to sixty-seven)	$37,680 in 2009	Your benefits are reduced by $1 for every $3 earned over the limit.
Over full retirement age	No limit	No impact

Social Security retirement benefits are income-tax-free for many people and partially tax-free for everyone else.

Individuals and families whose income is greater than set limits (refer to Social Security and IRS sources) may have up to 85 percent of their benefits subject to income tax. The actual calculation of the amount of benefits subject to income tax is fairly complex. A good rule of thumb is that if an individual's income is below $25,000 or a couple's income is below $32,000 (these limits assume 50 percent of your income comes from Social Security) there is likely to be no income tax on benefits received. It is not possible to know for certain what income tax rates will be in the future, but unless your family income is apt to be more than $40,000 to $50,000, your income tax rate is likely to be pretty modest.

When and how does Social Security get taxed, you ask? The computation, like all Internal Revenue Service requirements, is a tad complicated. In fact, they have a special worksheet just for that purpose. The math starts with your Adjusted Gross Income (AGI). To that you add one-half of all Social Security benefits and all unearned income received during the year. The latter almost always comes from tax-exempt interest received from municipal bonds (a favorite retiree investment). If the computed total is larger than $25,000 (single) or $32,000 (married filing jointly), then up to 50 percent of the Social Security benefit will be taxed. If the amount is larger than $34,000 (single) or $44,000 (married filing jointly), then up to 85 percent of the Social Security benefit will be taxed. To determine the exact amount that will be taxed, you must complete the handy-dandy worksheet supplied by the IRS for that purpose. Doesn't that sound like fun?

Fun or not, it is still a drill all those who draw Social Security payments must perform. Let's look at an example of a retired couple, John and Mary, who have the following joint income for 1999:

- Pensions and taxable investments $29,500
- Municipal bond interest $2,000
- Social Security benefit $14,000

In this scenario, their preliminary AGI consists of their pension and their taxable investment income, or $29,500. To that number, they must add their tax-free municipal bond interest ($2,000) and one-half of their Social Security benefits ($7,000). The resulting sum determines if any of the Social Security benefits will be taxed, and it will give John and Mary their modified adjusted gross income for the Social Security taxation test. If the sum exceeds either the $32,000 or the $44,000 threshold, then part of the Social Security will be taxed. Here's how it works:

- Preliminary adjusted gross income $29,500
- Tax-free municipal bond interest $2,000
- 50 percent of Social Security benefits $7,000
- Modified adjusted gross income $38,500
- Less first threshold amount $32,000
- Excess over first threshold $6,500

John and Mary have exceeded the first test threshold (but not the second), so now they must determine what part of their Social Security benefit will get taxed as ordinary income. That amount is the smaller of one-half of the excess determined above or one-half of the Social Security benefit received during the year. One-half of the excess is $3,250 ($6,500 divided by two). One-half of the benefit is $7,000 ($14,000 divided by two). Since, last time we checked, $3,250 is smaller than $7,000; $3,250 is the amount of John and Mary's Social Security benefit that must be declared as taxable income. That brings their reportable AGI to a total of $32,750 ($29,500 plus $3,250).

Didn't I tell you this was fun? But wait! There's more. Let's change things by making John and Mary 70½ years old, the age at which mandatory minimum required withdrawals must begin from traditional IRAs and qualified retirement plans. They hadn't touched these accounts, but now they must. In fact, they had to take $10,000 this year, all of it taxable and all of it part of John and Mary's preliminary AGI. How does that alter the situation? Now their modified

AGI and the excess over the two applicable thresholds become:

- Preliminary adjusted gross income $39,500
- Tax-free municipal bond interest $2,000
- 50 percent of Social Security benefits $7,000
- Modified adjusted gross income $48,500
- Excess over the first threshold ($48,500-$32,000): $16,500
- Excess over the second threshold ($48,500-$44,000): $ 4,500

John and Mary must determine the smaller of:

- 50 percent of the excess over the $32,000 threshold, plus 35 percent of the excess over the $44,000 threshold [($16,500 × 0.5) + ($4,500 × 0.35)]: $ 9,825
- 85 percent of the Social Security benefit ($14,000 × 0.85): $11,900
- 50 percent of the Social Security benefit plus 85 percent of the excess over the $44,000 threshold [($14,000 × 0.5) + ($4,500 × 0.85)]: $10,825

The smallest of those three computations, or $9,825, now gets added to John and Mary's preliminary AGI of $39,500 to bring their reportable AGI to $49,325.

In the first case, John and Mary ended up with $3,250 in additional taxable income, and in the second example with $9,825 more. Did they plan for the tax on that income? If not, they could be in for a rude surprise. Not only will they pay more in income taxes, they may also be slapped with a penalty for a failure to pay enough estimated withholding taxes during the year. Estimated income taxes are not withheld from Social Security payments unless the recipient has submitted *Form W-4V (Voluntary Withholding Request)* to the Social Security Administration (SSA). In the absence of that action, recipients are responsible for those payments. Unless one of the limited safe-harbor tests is passed, failure to make quarterly payments will result in a penalty on top of the taxes due.

Didn't make quarterly payments during the year? Then you may be liable for an underpayment penalty due to insufficient withholdings in the first three quarters of this year when you received those Social Security benefits. But there is a loophole that might allow you to avoid that outcome. If you work part-time, you could ask your employer to withhold additional monies for income taxes for the rest of the year—up to 100 percent of your income if need be. Income tax payments withheld from your paycheck don't have to be made quarterly, and they will help offset the amount you may be penalized, for failing to make quarterly payments based on your Social Security checks.

Regardless of your situation this year, consider the potential of Social Security taxation. When you do your taxes for this year, run a pro forma tax return for next year's income. If you see that your Social Security benefit might get taxed, then either submit Form W-4V to the SSA or make your necessary quarterly estimated withholding payments unless you're absolutely sure you won't owe a penalty for not doing so.

MEDICARE

Title XVIII of the Social Security Act, entitled "Health Insurance for the Aged and Disabled," is commonly known as "Medicare." As part of the Social Security Amendments of 1965, the Medicare legislation established a health insurance program for aged persons to complement the retirement—survivors and disability insurance benefits under other titles of the Social Security Act.

When first implemented in 1966, Medicare covered most persons aged sixty-five and over. Since then, legislation has added other groups:

- Persons who are entitled to disability benefits for twenty-four months or more (1972)
- Persons with End-Stage Renal Disease (ESRD) requiring dialysis or kidney transplant (1972)
- Certain otherwise noncovered persons who elect to be covered under the Medicare program (1973)

Medicare consists of two parts:

1. Hospital Insurance (HI), also known as Part A
2. Supplementary Medical Insurance (SMI), also known as Part B

When Medicare began on July 1, 1966, there were 19.1 million persons enrolled in the program. By the end of 1966, 3.7 million persons had received at least some health care services covered by Medicare. In 1994, about 36.9 million persons were enrolled in one or both parts of the Medicare program. About 83 percent (84 percent of the aged) of all Medicare "Enrollees" used some HI and/or SMI service in FY 1994, and thus are the 1994 Medicare "Beneficiaries."

Medicare benefits are divided into two parts.

Part A primarily covers inpatient hospital, skilled nursing facility care, and home health care. Once enrolled in Medicare, you will receive these benefits automatically and do not pay premiums for them (you've already paid for them through your taxes).

When you apply for Part A, you can enroll into Part B. This second part covers most doctors' bills, as well as some medical services and supplies. You can turn down Part B if you choose because it requires a monthly premium. It is critical that you sign up for Medicare when eligible at age sixty-five. Otherwise, you will be penalized for signing up late, and the penalty will be in the form of significantly higher Part B premiums.

We do not address Medicare Part D, the drug care part of the plan because of its complexity and urge you to consult a Medicare Specialist.

Medigap insurance gives benefits that Parts A and B don't offer. This kind of health coverage is sold by private companies specifically to complement Medicare insurance.

If you choose to have your Medicare medical services provided by a health maintenance organization (HMO), you may not need to consider Medigap insurance.

Medicare applications are handled through your local Social Security office and are usually submitted when you apply for Social Security. To ensure that your entrance into Medicare is problem-free, you should contact your local Social Security office within three months before you turn sixty-five. If you fail to enroll within this three-month period, you'll have to pay a penalty for late enrollment. This time frame is important particularly for those who have retired or plan to retire before age sixty-five.

Medicare becomes effective for people following the regular application process on the first day of the month, in which they turn sixty-five.

Medicare provides 100 percent of expenses for the first twenty days of skilled nursing care after three consecutive days of hospitalization, not including the day of discharge. This nursing care must be physician-prescribed to be covered by Medicare. For days twenty-one to one hundred in a skilled nursing facility, the beneficiary must pay a co-payment. Beginning from day 101, you are responsible for the costs yourself.

Planning and Action

Do you know what the survival rate of airplane accidents is? You won't believe it. Take a guess right now. I bet you won't be anywhere close.

On average, ninety-six out of every one hundred people involved in airplane mishaps survive the ordeal. Amazing, isn't it? Even with serious accidents, as long as there was some chance of surviving, three-quarters of the passengers gets out alive.

And here's another shocker. Many of the people who do perish could have survived, but didn't. So what makes the difference? If you guessed panic, you'd be wrong. Yes, panic kills, but it almost never happens in desperate situations like airplane disasters, earthquakes, or terrorist attacks like 9/11.

Most people don't panic. They freeze. They do nothing, because they don't know what to do. And that's what kills them. Usually, two things make the difference between life and death: planning and action.

Since I learned those statistics, my preparation at the beginning of flights has completely changed. Before, I never paid attention to things like exits, flight attendant emergency instructions, or reviewing the safety card. What was the point? If something went wrong, I figured, I was a goner anyway.

Now I know differently. I note my exits and try to get a seat close to one (seats two to five rows away are the safest). I review the safety card so I know how each emergency exit door on the plane works. I am fully alert with my seatbelt tight and my shoes on during the most vulnerable times—the first three and the last eight minutes of any flight.

And I have a plan in case something goes wrong, a plan I review every flight at take-off and just before landing.

Here's the point: Our preparation is different when we have an expectation that preparation will make a difference. And when we have a plan, we are more likely to act.[17]

At this point in the book, we covered the concept of establishing financial goals, developing a plan to get to those goals, and the need to assess your current situation and how far down the road you have to go. It's a bit daunting taking all this information in at the same time. You probably feel like that person that starts a new diet plan with all the intentions to eat right and exercise regularly. You study all the ideas on what to eat and how often to eat it. You learn how to mix strength training with cardiovascular types of exercising. Then the reality hits you, it is simple to say you want to be healthier and not easy to actually follow through. This is why you need a coach. Also, it is good because your awareness has woken up. Your consciousness about your financial future has been shaken out of its trance, "that everything will take care of itself." And now you're saying to yourself, "What do I do?" How can you realistically hope to make your goals become reality now? Read on, help is on the way!

Part II
Financial Gravity

Three Rules for Success

Gravity is a strange force in the universe. It has always been there and it affects so many things we do. Did you know gravity is actually necessary for flight? Ask an engineer if you are having trouble sleeping and you will hear all about concepts like lift and thrust. Without gravity we would float (like the astronauts). It is the invisible force that holds the world together. It's odd that something that literally holds the world together and makes life possible had to be "discovered." Realistically, it was always there all along! The rules weren't codified, but they were there. You jumped, you fell. Speed increases down a hill, and going up a hill took more energy. These all existed before the "discovery" of gravity. Apples fell long before the one that hit Isaac Newton on the head.

The bottom line is that even after gravity was discovered, people had three choices: Believe it existed and follow the rules; be apathetic and not care about the rules, or don't believe in the rules at all. Regardless of people's responses to the new and codified rules, they existed nonetheless. If someone jumped off a building and screamed, "I don't believe in gravity!" it didn't help. The fact is, he would still end in a thud on the ground below.

So why the science lesson in a financial book? Because the three rules I am going to introduce are Financial Gravity. Regardless of how you respond to the rules, they will be there. You can think some newfangled smart guy has figured out how to subvert the rules, but just like gravity you will feel a thud at some point, and it will be your finances/ portfolio. In a strange irony, this shock is sometimes followed by jumping out of real buildings as well. So you can choose to ignore what you are about to read, but these three rules are the heart and soul of financial planning success. They are the flour, sugar, and eggs in the cake, the spices in your stew. They permeate everything you do financially, and you ignore them only at your peril. You will be able to use these rules to choose advisors, to make many, many financial decisions that reach beyond the distribution planning scope of this book. First, let's talk about credit.

YOUR CREDIT SCORE

Your credit score, or FICO, has a huge impact on the interest rates, for which you are eligible for loans and credit cards. An improvement of just fifty points in your score can mean paying hundreds of dollars less per month for a five-year auto loan, for example. Understanding what makes up your FICO score is the first step toward improving it so that you can later frame this score for prominent display in your home, but I am getting ahead of myself.

The Big Three credit reporting agencies (viz., Equifax, Transunion, and Experian) calculate your FICO, or credit score, based upon the same formula. The creators of the FICO score formula, the Fair, Isaac & Company, do not make the exact formula public. But they have made public the five main elements of your credit score and how heavily each component is weighted mathematically to get your total score. The breakdown is as follows (note: this information is subject to change at any time, so be sure to check the Fair, Isaac & Company Web site or recent press releases for the most up-to-date information):

> **Payment history—35 percent (of Score)—**Of course, if you have never made any late payments on any of your accounts, the payment history portion of your score should look quite attractive. Items in your past that can bring down this part of your score are: bankruptcies,

law suits, and wage attachments. Ideally you want to have a long history of consistently paying on time and you want to make sure that you are carrying a balance of some kind at all times. (That is you need to have a long history of profitability for the credit grantors to score well here; profitability to credit grantors is the key)

Capacity Amounts owed—30 percent—This element boils down to the ratio of *the amount you owe* to *the amount of credit extended to you.* For example, if you have multiple credit cards with a total of $20,000 in credit lines, but you owe a total of $10,000 on those cards, your ratio is 50 percent. The lower your ratio, the better it is for your score. Also factored into this element is the number of credit accounts you now have opened. The Big three credit agencies like you to have at least a few accounts open, but at the same time not too many. They want you to carry a lot of debt, but not too much. They want you to get close to your credit limit, but not too close. (This was mentioned in the previous payment history section)

Length of credit history—15 percent—This component actually factors on two items: the total length of your credit history *and* the average length of time your current accounts have been open. In both cases, the longer, the better, in terms of your credit score. (see previous two i.e.,)

New credit—10 percent—Avoid applying for multiple new credit cards or loans at once if you are trying to improve your credit score. Instead, take your time and slowly build up a history with each loan instrument one at a time before applying for the next. (The point is that while credit grantors want you to carry lots of debt for a long time, they just don't want you to get it all at once. So have lots of debt, just don't look like you need it! Acquiring it all at once would make you look desperate and that is a red flag.

Types of credit used—10 percent—Making regular and on-time payments to multiple lenders can help your credit score. For example, a mix of revolving credit cards, charge cards, installment debt, and store charge accounts is ideal. Again, having multiple types of credit is only useful if you keep the balances low, relative to your total credit line. (i.e., the credit grantors don't like people that play favorites and spread your wealth around, otherwise you will be labeled a credit bigot and nobody wants that!)

By remaining aware of what elements the Big Three credit reporting agencies take into account when calculating your FICO score, you will be empowered to make adjustments to your financial life and improve your score.

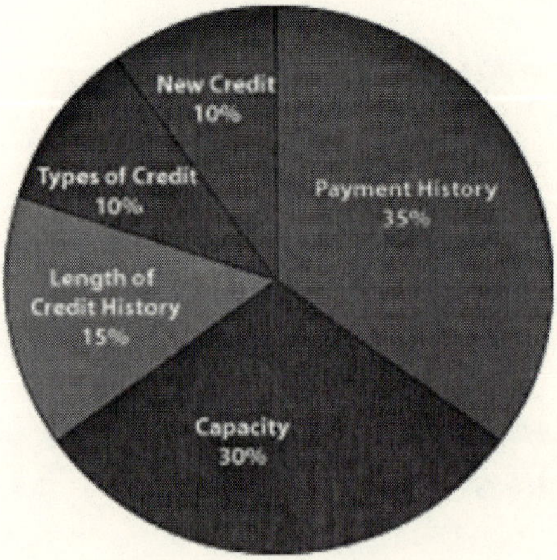

Here is an ideal example: you acquire a bunch of credit. You want one of each; Discover, MasterCard, Visa, and American Express. You will want to have at least one premium card with an important-sounding color, like gold or platinum or MasterCard Black. You need to acquire these over a long period of time, say ten years. Use what I call the 10/10/10 rule. ten types of credit, over ten years, 10 percent shy of being maxed out.

Once you have achieved this, you will want to order your credit report from all three agencies. Your score should be in the 750 plus range (this is an exceptional score). I would have the scores printed on parchment paper (makes it look old, like it has been this way a long time) and then you can go to any quality framing shop to have them mount these three scores in something like a montage (consult Martha Stewart magazine you got with your credit card for ideas).

Once you have completed this, mount it someplace so that everyone coming to your house can see it! Congratulations! You have just achieved financial slavery, but you have a nice wall-hanging and you can brag about your great score.

You are probably wondering why I have spent so much time talking about the FICO score. Think of the debt culture we live in as "brine" that you are soaking in. It permeates all that we do. Soaking the Thanksgiving turkey in brine is a good thing (we tried it one year, and it was fantastic), however living in a "brine" of the debt culture has been devastating. Many of you were reading the information on improving your FICO score as if it is really important because the cultural advertising messages and sales pitches continue to tell us this. If you did not catch my "tongue-in-cheek" humor, let me enlighten you. Your goal should not be to have a good FICO score, it should be to have no debt. The only score that matters is zero debt. Focus on that! If you still think zero is not your target than *you are* a turkey and you know what happens to them after they have been soaked in brine long enough!

No matter what you do, it "appears" that the only way to get ahead is to use debt. Financial books call it "other people's money" or OPM. It has other fancy names like leveraging. But it is all debt and it is bad. Like gravity you can ignore it, but it will eventually catch up to you. Even repackaging debt instruments and renaming them something clever like Mortgage Backed Securities has caught up to us and melted down the world economy. Wall Street, governments, and individuals all were sucked into the debt trap we have all paid for their collective mistakes. It is easy to point at someone else's mistakes while we ignore the exact same mistake (albeit with less zeros behind the numbers) with our own finances.

I am always stunned when a couple with $150,000 in unsecured debt tells me how happy they are that they have a FICO score above seven hundred. Talking about losing your perspective! The FICO score in my opinion is a target that says to the credit industry that *you* are what they want, which is a profitable client. *You don't want to be a profitable client to the credit industry*! My suggestion is use the above list to *lower* your score. A person with no mortgage, no debt, and no available credit will not have as high of a score as someone dutifully servicing debt. Do you want to have $150,000 in debt with a high score or no debt and a low score. Bottom line, most people have the wrong goal. Ignore the FICO score, it is *not* a badge of honor like most people treat it.

RULE #1: PAY OFF ALL DEBT

You cannot borrow your way to prosperity, only to the illusion of prosperity, and it is a fleeting illusion.

DEBT DEFINED—THE AMERICAN CULTURE HAS COLLAPSED

There are about three things that have come together that have caused today's dilemma with debt. One is that we live in the most marketed-to culture in the history of the world. We are sold a lot of stuff and, so, we buy a lot of stuff. Can you picture a day in the week when you don't spend money at all?

The second thing is that one of the most heavily marketed products in this heavily marketed-to culture is debt. Debt is no longer a result of a commitment to buy a product or service; it's a product in and of itself that is sold with great energy, with great financial backing and with great sophistication. Financial institutions do an efficient job, sending out six billion credit card offers to consumers each year.

So, if you combine these two things, a lot of marketing with a lot of marketing of debt, and then add "Easy payments" with an ever-decreasing attention span and immaturity—you put all that together and you have an increasingly disastrous situation. We definitely have, as a society incrementally, degree by degree, gotten deeper in debt every year.

For today's generation, debt may seem to be a necessary evil of the modern life. You can't get a decent education without it. No one can realistically purchase a new car absent financing. And 99 percent of home buyers require preapproved debt commitments to even get in the door. As we noted before, the cost of living makes it very difficult, if not impossible, for many people today to live cash in hand 100 percent of the time. In any case, there are some basic things to remember about debt:[18]

People are loaded with credit card debt. The average household with at least one credit card has nearly $9,200 in credit card debt and the average interest rate runs in the mid to high teens at any given time. It is not uncommon to see interest rates in the mid 20 percent, and people wonder why it is hard to get ahead.

Some debt is utilitarian. Borrowing *responsibly* for a home or college *usually* makes good sense because these are typically appreciating assets; your home and you (or potentially your children's future). This, however, is still dangerous because of the general impact of debt. Few things have better long-term implications than a good education and a place to live. One just needs to be very careful because it is easy to get carried away in both of these areas. Debt has the tendency to be like salty snacks, it is hard to eat just one. Then you justify bad behavior by saying, "A potato chip is a vegetable, right?" There is a difference between an investment and a good purchase. Your home is not an investment, but it could be a good purchase.

Just think that all debt is bad, and you can stay out of a lot of trouble. Don't use a credit card to pay for things you consume quickly, such as meals and vacations, if you can't afford to pay off your monthly bill in full, in a month, then, there's no faster way to fall into debt.

The financial side is easy to quantify, and the numbers are huge. Americans are drowning in debt, carrying a record $972.5 billion in revolving charges at the end of 2007, according to the data from the Federal Reserve. The average household has $11,000 to $12,000 in credit card debt. Those figures are diluted by those who don't hold any debt.

Households that carry debt from month to month carry close to $17,000 of unsecured debt on average.[19]

Cheryl Allebrand says one out of every five households is either behind on payments or over the limit on at least one account. Up and down every street in America, you go to every fifth house, and they're living in the penalty rate zone on credit cards. To put things in perspective, she calculates that the interest and penalties alone on a debt of $17,000 totals $400 a month. The first $400 they send doesn't pay down the $17,000.[20]

The causes can be lumped into a couple of common categories of mistake:[21]

- **Reduced income/same expenses**—We often delay bringing expenses in line with a reduction in income for a host of good reasons and let debt fill the gap. The sooner you adjust to your new reality, whether it be temporary or permanent, the better off you'll be.
- **Divorce**—More than half do it, some more than once. I can think of few things more expensive and likely to put you in debt. For those of you who have never experienced a divorce and would like to get some idea of the impact, sell all your assets and get the money in $50 bills. Go to a hotel on a busy street, and you and your spouse open two windows and see who can throw the most money out the fastest. It can be breathtaking.
- **Poor money management**—A monthly spending plan is essential. Without one, you have no idea where your money is going. You may be spending hundreds of dollars unnecessarily each month and end up having to charge purchases, on which you should have spent that money. Planning is no more difficult than writing down your expenses and income and reconciling the two. You will be surprised at how powerful you'll feel when you are making thoughtful decisions about where and when to spend your money.

- **Underemployment**—People who experience underemployment may continue to think of it as only temporary or if they are coming off unemployment feel a false sense of relief. Yes, you deserve a break, but this is not the time to increase spending. Get those expenses in line with your current income. Down the road, if you increase your income due to more hours, a second job, or a better job, then that is the time to start adding in some of the previous spending before you became underemployed.
- **Gambling**—Call it America's new entertainment or (considering the boom in tribal casinos) the Indian's revenge. Either way, there is a guaranteed exchange of money from you to "The house." It can be addictive, hard to stop, and loans are freely available. Gambling establishments may be the only place you can mortgage your house while intoxicated and have it be legal. I'm sorry, I forgot—this is entertainment!
- **Medical expenses**—Gaps in coverage, lapsed policies, and increasingly costly alternatives make this a popular category. Just about every doctor I know now takes credit cards. If you think it's for convenience, think again. The medical industry wants to get paid at the time, service is rendered. They know that if they don't, the chances of their getting paid drops. This means more debt for you, less for them. To be fair, they are not in the lending business, but this only masks a bigger problem.
- **Saving too little or not at all**—The simplest way to avoid unwanted debt is to prepare for unexpected expenditures by saving three to six months of living expenses. With a savings cushion in place, a job layoff, illness, or divorce will not cause immediate financial strain and increase debt. You always hear, "Pay yourself first." Do it, and it will grow and be there when you need it. No one has ever regretted having a savings cushion. Some things need to be repeated because they can't be said enough. Saving money is one of those concepts.

- **No-money communication skills**—It is important to communicate with your spouse or significant other and your children about finances. Keep the lines of communication open and discuss financial goals and spending styles. If you are married to a spender and you are a saver, you will want to map out a strategy for you both, to get what you want. Know what credit accounts you each have and promise each other to be honest about what each other spends. Many people find out that their spouses have racked up thousands of dollars in credit card debt and they had no idea that the accounts even existed. This often leads to divorce, a problem listed above.
- **Banking on a windfall**—Spending tomorrow's money today is very tempting. Especially, if you believe that tomorrow will come no matter what, a planned job bonus may not be a sure thing. The inheritance that you believe will come your way, may not. A tax refund. The lesson is, don't spend the money until the check clears.
- **Financial illiteracy**—Many people don't understand how money works and grows, how to save and invest for a rainy day, or even why they should balance their checkbook. The schools don't teach it, your parents may not have sat you down and explained it. It doesn't matter. You are responsible for your life and your money anyway. Financial mistakes are increasingly expensive and complicated to resolve. Get educated and get in control. Reading this book will help, but of course at this point if you have read this far, I am "Preaching to the choir."
- **Thinking you don't need help**—People seek and pay for the advice and services for their plumbing, air conditioning, yard, garage doors, electrical amenities, health, etc., but neglect to seek the advice in the one area that pays for the services of all the others.

More and more, people are unfortunately finding themselves sinking deeper into the debt quagmire. There is a simple (but not easy) system of managing debt repayments. You can actually tackle debt problems without damaging your credit rating. The system, called the debt snowball, has been popularized by Dave Ramsey and goes against the grain of most of the advice given by self-help books and many financial advisors.

Many debt counselors now advise paying more money toward the debts carrying the highest interest rates first, with the lower interest rate debts receiving the minimum payments. This is mathematically the best way to reduce debt. But, it is also "Treating the symptom, not the disease" as the saying goes. Most debt is a result of a lot of psychological factors. Since the "Disease" is psychological, then the cure needs to be addressed psychologically as well. In many cases the debt that has the highest interest rate also has the highest amount outstanding and it can *feel* (psychologically and emotionally) that no matter how much money you plough into clearing the debt, it never seems to get lower. By paying the minimum amounts to your other debts, you'd be hard pushed to make a dent in them too!

However, according to Dave Ramsey, John Pollock, and smarter and more handsome people than both of us, the best method is to create a debt snowball by actually paying off the smallest debt first! The method works by setting aside a fixed amount of money that will allow you to cover all your debts with a little extra leftover. Then you pay the minimum payment to everything other than the smallest balance, where you devote whatever cash you have set aside toward the debt. Once that debt is cleared, move on to the next smallest account, add the payment you were paying on the smallest account onto the minimum payment for the next smallest debt and continue the minimum payments for the others. As each debt becomes cleared, the snowball of cash you can pay toward your debt gets bigger, and as you get toward the bigger debts, the snowball will allow you to pay more to each debt and clear it off quicker. The mathematics may be slightly (very slightly) slower than paying off the highest interest, but it is like a diet where you don't see any weight loss for weeks; you are likely to get discouraged and quit. You need the early emotional and psychological boost from actually losing weight soon in the new and painful endeavor. The same goes for debt reduction. The psychological benefit of paying off that first debt no matter how small, will give you the mental momentum you need to tackle the next one and this will give you a much better shot at success.

The system works, regardless of who you have debt with: banks, credit card issuers, debt collection agencies, car financing, etc. Before long you'll *see* and *feel* debt being reduced far more than you would if you tackled your bigger balances that have higher interest rates. So, if you're struggling with debt, a debt snowball might be the answer; it starts with a list of debts, their balances, and the minimum payment. There are many Web sites available, which can provide calculators to help you work out the size of the snowball you'll need to help you get out of debt, as well as help with laying out the process of making it happen.

The Snowball Recipe:

- **Ingredient 1**—set aside a fixed amount of money that will allow you to cover all your debts with a little extra leftover.
- **Ingredient 2**—you pay the minimum payment to everything other than the smallest balance, where you devote whatever cash you have set aside toward paying down that specific debt.
- **Ingredient 3**—once the target debt is cleared on the smallest account, add the payment you were paying on the smallest account onto the minimum payment for the next smallest debt.
- **Ingredient 4**—continues the minimum payments for the others until debt-free.

WHY A MORTGAGE IS NOT A TRUE TAX DEDUCTION AND OTHER MORTGAGE MYTHS

The term "Mortgage" comes from the Old French "Dead pledge," apparently meaning that the pledge ends (dies) either when the obligation is fulfilled or the property is taken through foreclosure. P.

We noted earlier that a mortgage is usually classified as a "Good" type of debt. These are the debts we take on to get ahead in life. The reason real estate is worth getting into debt for is that, historically, real estate tends to appreciate in value enough to sell and leverage into better real estate. The average family up to now usually lives in at least two homes before settling down in the house they will have for their life, after retirement. At each step, the goal is to use the existing home to build capital to get to a desired home in the future. Therefore, a mortgage is the means to get started in real estate in the first place. In fact, it's the only way for many since almost all of us don't have the cash to purchase our first house upfront.

A mortgage itself is the transfer of an interest in property to a lender as a security for a debt, usually a loan of money. While a mortgage in itself is not a debt, it is lender's security for a debt. It is a transfer of an interest in land (or the equivalent), from the owner to the mortgage lender, on the condition that this interest will be returned to the owner of the real estate when the terms of the mortgage have been satisfied or performed. In other words, the mortgage is a security for the loan that the lender makes to the borrower. Note that the mortgage is a stream of money (principle and interest) going back to the lender (mortgagor or mortgage grantor) from the borrower (mortgagee). In other words, the money is granted only when you can show the ability to pay the stream of money, and is secured by the house, but the real security in the ability to repay. (This simple rule was suspended for about a decade when the government decided to ignore the "Laws of financial gravity" and governed based on their feelings instead of math and economics. The year 2008 produced the mortgage "Meltdown," which was the outcome of violating the natural laws of economics.)

So what are the benefits of paying down the mortgage debt? Isn't it a tax deduction we want to keep as long as possible? Yes, you do get a tax deduction for the amount of interest you pay on a mortgage debt. To some, this gives the appearance that you're then getting the interest back at the end of the year. That's not quite true.

An income tax deduction for homeownership is sacred in Americans' minds, but often the deduction doesn't add up to much. The amount of interest and taxes typically paid on a median-priced home in the U.S. results in unimpressive tax benefits. If you live in the Midwest, are in the 25 percent tax bracket, and you have 20 percent equity in your median-priced home, there are possibly no tax benefits at all.

Uncle Sam's standard deduction of $10,700 in 2007 for a married couple filing jointly—available whether you own a home or not—exceeds the value of the mortgage interest and tax deductions from the very first day of homeownership for vast number of people.

In 2006, the national median home sales price was $222,000. With a 20 percent equity stake and a thirty-year mortgage loan at 6 percent, in the first year, the tax benefit is an estimated $1,195. The value of the deduction for a couple in the 25 percent tax bracket declines every year, until the thirteenth year, when it's worth a grand total of $3.

In lower-priced areas, it gets worse. Married taxpayers in Akron, Ohio, who own a regional median-price house worth $110,200, mortgaged with 20 percent equity, and who are in the 25 percent tax bracket would receive zero tax benefits from day one.

The picture changes dramatically for a single homeowner with a house in San Francisco, with a median price of $733,400. In the first year of a home purchase, for which he puts down 3 percent, the tax benefit would be worth $17,632. If that homeowner, in the 33 percent tax bracket, were to hold on to his home for thirty years, the cumulative deduction would be worth $444,403.

This is a pretty good deal. Or is it?

The "tax benefit" is the deduction *over* the standard deduction, which would produce a refund that would be for $5,818. This would seem to be substantial, but what happened to the other $11,813? It is gone! The bank gets it. So you give the bank $17,632 and get $5,818 back from the federal government. I have a better idea, one that benefits both of us. Send me the $17,632, and I will send *you* $11,813 and I will keep the $5,818! We both win, you get double the original tax deduction, and I get $5,818 for giving you such stellar advice. The only loser is the banking industry.

Is carrying a mortgage into retirement something that most people should seek to avoid? The answer is a slam dunk. *yes*! However, if you are not convinced yet, that it is a bad idea from the tax perspective to keep a mortgage, here are even more reasons why you should pay it off, and one reason you might want to add it back on!

One altruistic benefit is that you can actually leave a house, not a debt, to your heirs. If you want to leave the house to your children or someone else who doesn't have a lot of resources, do them a favor and pay off the mortgage. Otherwise, they may be faced with selling the house whether they want to or not.

You also protect yourself from suit. In many states, if you're sued, your home is exempt from judgment. Owning your home outright also can provide some protection from bankruptcy. One hopes sheltering assets in your home will never pay off, but it's something to consider.

Make a sure bet. Gillette Edmunds, author of *Retire on the House*, a book about real estate investing, pooh-poohs the notion that it is smarter to keep a mortgage and invest at a higher interest rate. “The problem is that mortgage interest is a sure thing and the investment isn’t,” he says. “You could lose everything you invested and still have to pay the mortgage.”

Cash flow Equivalent Return

I would like to expand on Mr. Edmund’s quote by exploring a concept called cash flow equivalent return.

When you move into your retirement years, you no longer will live off the cash flow that you generate by working, but you will live off the cash flow of Social Security, pensions, and your assets. This makes the idea of cash flow equivalent returns even more important. Assume you have a $100,000 mortgage. In this illustration, you have an equal amount in savings ($100,000) and your monthly payment is $1,000 in principle and interest payment. We will ignore the taxes and insurance because those will exist after the mortgage is paid off.

The dilemma is what to do with the $100,000 mortgage. Typically when seeking advice with this type of question, there are three places and people who tend to go for answers. The first is a “Tax advisor.” This is either a CPA, a Certified Public *Accountant* (note the emphasis on the word, accountant) or the person that prepared your taxes. Just like the problem, we outline later where the “Advisor” is really just a person working in a “Retail outlet” with a selection of products in their inventory, therefore the advice you are given is based on the “Inventory” of the “Store.” The problem in this case is not with inventory movement or sales (at least not in the area of accounting/tax advice), but a problem of function and objectives. Whoever does your taxes typically has two goals, one, get all the information you give them in the right spot and the other to get you a refund. The bigger the refund, the happier you are with them and you will come back. The problem with both these objectives is that neither of their objectives serves your overall goals. They may serve your immediate goals. For example, eating a whole cheesecake in a single sitting may accomplish my immediate desire, something good to eat, but may not accomplish my overall long-term goal of weight loss. The tax preparer cares only that you are happy now with the tax refund (cheesecake), they will not connect the now desire (cheesecake) with the long-term objective of retirement (weight loss).

All of this to say that if you ask a tax preparer if you should take $100,000 out of a savings account to pay off your single greatest (potentially greatest as we have already discussed) tax write off, they automatically flash forward to a year from now when they are doing your tax return and you are upset because your "Taxes went up and they have never been this high before!" All of a sudden the change in your tax status becomes their fault and they lose a client. Once they snap back to reality from the vision of the future they say calmly and with authority, "You don't want to pay off your mortgage; it is your biggest tax deduction." Add to this, the fact that it is safer, for them, to suggest you follow a course you are already on, then to suggest a change of any kind, and you have the answer before you ask it.

I know what most are thinking, "But, I just wanted their unbiased opinion of what I should do." If you want an unbiased opinion of what you should do and you want it to relate to your overall objectives and goals, it will take time and that kind of advice is not free. Sometimes "Free" costs you far more in the long run.

So the first professional you typically go to for advice is no help on what you should do with the $100,000 and whether or not to pay off your home, so the next person is the banker/ broker/insurance agent. Since we will deal with this later (look for BBQ analogy), we will not explore this now. Finally, what might be the worst of the group is relying on friends, family, and yourself. Maybe you will stumble into good advice, but the odds are against it. First your friends and family will advise on what they have done and that has no relation to the situation you are in. Second, misery loves company, or in other words, they are pretty sure, the path they have taken is right, but whether it is right or not they are going to want someone else doing the same dumb thing they are doing.

When it comes to you, "Listening," you have some issues to deal with yourself. The first is can you keep your emotions and long-held opinions in check? In my experience, the answer to this is always, no. The second is, are you really looking for advice, or are you looking for an accomplice (the accomplice is easier to find with friends and family than with a true professional)? Once I had a gentleman and his wife in my office. He immediately sat down and proceeded to tell me everything he was doing right, in his own eyes. After yielding the floor for several minutes I had to interrupt. I bluntly asked, "Are you looking for advice or an accomplice?" He was stunned because he was used to meeting with sales people who would not dare offend him and risk a loss of a potential sale. His wife immediately laughed. He was not amused, but asked what I meant. I told him his figures were wrong in three areas that he had shown me, and he had been talking for just a few minutes.

He had been convinced by his worst enemy (himself, he was an engineer and this is very common among engineers) that the $125k in CDs earning 6 percent and the mortgage that was $115k at 5.75 percent was a net gain because of the difference in interest and the tax deduction he was getting. So where were the errors? The CDs were being taxed at his income tax bracket of 25 percent and only half of his mortgage payment was being deducted because of the standard deduction issue we have discussed. So he was actually losing money every year. I was able to clearly show him, using his numbers and his tax returns, that he was making a mistake that was costing him money. But he was looking for an accomplice, so he did not listen and did not change. I have countless stories similar to this. If the gentleman had chosen to listen, I would have further shown him that he was neglecting the principle of cash flow equivalent return.

Using the numbers I introduced, a few paragraphs back, I would have shown him that a mortgage payment costing $1,000 a month is negative cash flow. If the mortgage is $100,000 and I have $100,000 in the bank, I can easily figure out what my $100,000 would need to earn in order to create the positive cash flow necessary to make my monthly payment. $1,000 month × 12 = $12,000 a year. This means I would need $12,000 in interest on your investment or a 12 percent return, guaranteed each year to make my mortgage payments.

Wait, there is more, the 12 percent is the net of taxes. I need to get to 15 percent to offset the 25 percent in federal taxes and that does not count state taxes! So you need a cash flow equivalent return of 15 percent, guaranteed! So my conclusion is, *pay off your house now*!

For most people, paying off the mortgage has the intangible advantage of creating peace of mind, something that I would consider very tangible. Being debt-free including the mortgage has psychological benefits that are enormous! *No one* ever regrets getting debt-free. *No one* ever regrets paying off a mortgage.

When would you want to consider getting back into a mortgage? I realize that there are circumstances that derail your plans, or you may be reading saying that it is too late for you. If in later years, everything does not go as planned then you can tap into the equity you created. We will discuss this next.

Reverse Mortgages

Many retired individuals find themselves living on a fixed income. Many also own a home, which is either paid for, or has a very small mortgage, a situation often described as "house-rich-and-cash-poor." In the past, there have been few acceptable ways to take advantage of this home equity, apart from selling the home. Recently, however, a new financial tool has been developed—the Reverse Mortgage—which provides qualified individuals, access to the equity in their homes, and still permits them to retain ownership of the home.

WHAT IS A REVERSE MORTGAGE?

Most homeowners are familiar with the traditional home mortgage. An individual buys a home, and, over time, as the monthly payments are made, the balance due on the mortgage is gradually reduced. A homeowner's equity—the difference between what is owed and the market value, is also increased if a home's market value increases. In the traditional, "Forward" mortgage, as debt decreases, equity increases.

A "Reverse" mortgage, as the name implies, works in the other direction. With a reverse mortgage, cash flows from a lender to a borrower. Over time the balance due increases. In a reverse mortgage, as debt increases, equity decreases.

- Eligibility—reverse mortgage programs generally require that all borrowers be at least sixty-two years of age. The home must be owner-occupied, and be the borrower's principal residence. Not all types of homes qualify; all programs accept single-family-detached homes, and some allow two- to four-unit owner-occupied homes, condominiums, and manufactured homes. Only first mortgages are permitted. Any other debt secured by the home must either be first paid off, or paid off with proceeds from the reverse mortgage. If the house is brand new, it will have to be "Seasoned" for one year before a reverse mortgage can be placed on it. If the house is in a trust, it will have to be titled back to the individual.

(Depending on the state, this could be a problem, so seek advice)

- Ownership—during the term of the mortgage, the borrower remains the owner of the home, and is responsible for payment of property taxes, maintenance and repair, and keeping the home insured.
- Repayment—no payments are required as long as the borrower lives in the home. The outstanding loan balance, including accrued interest and any loan costs, is due when the last borrower sells the home, permanently leaves, or dies. In a few instances, the loan is due at the end of a fixed term. Typically, the loan is repaid by either selling or refinancing the home. Any remaining equity is paid to the borrower, the borrower's estate, or heirs.
- Maximum loan balance—a borrower can never owe more than the value of the home at the time the loan is repaid. Reverse mortgages are generally *nonrecourse loans*, which means, the lender can only look to the value of the home for repayment.

THE PROS AND CONS OF REVERSE MORTGAGES

There are a number of reasons why a reverse mortgage may not be appropriate:

- Not needed—some retired individuals will not want to consider a reverse mortgage simply because it is not needed; their financial needs during retirement are already adequately met. This is the goal.
- Security—reflecting long-held attitudes toward savings and debt, some individuals may not be comfortable with the idea of placing any type of mortgage on the home, once it is paid for, which I would agree with except when faced with common sense problems.
- Legacy for heirs—rather than using the equity in the home for current needs, a homeowner may want the equity to pass to family members or other beneficiaries, such as a charity.

There are also a number of situations where a reverse mortgage can help:

- Breathing Room—for some, the extra dollars provided by a reverse mortgage may make it easier to pay routine monthly expenses. For others, it may allow an occasional "Splurge . . ." unless splurging has got you in this mess in the first place.
- Pay off debt—funds from a reverse mortgage can be used to pay off other types of personal debt that require monthly payments, such as credit card balances. Cash flow is king in retirement.
- Maintain independence—some may wish to make improvements to the home, or pay for in-home care, to allow them to remain independent as long as possible.
- Provide for the future—even though the present financial situation is stable, a reverse mortgage can provide a way to meet unforeseen future circumstances. This should be used as a last resort.
- Replace—if you are paying on a "Forward" mortgage and you have about 50 percent equity (this is a consistent rule of thumb) you may be able to get a reverse mortgage and eliminate your monthly payments. You will not get the typical cash out like you would if it was paid off, but you will improve cash flow.

CHOOSING A REVERSE MORTGAGE

Unlike just a few years ago, a wide range of reverse mortgage programs are available today. Further, the specific details of each program can vary greatly. A standard series of questions can be used to compare and contrast each program:

- How much cash?—In general, the amount of cash, which can be borrowed will depend on the lender's policies, the age of the borrowers, the value of the home, the home's condition and location, and the interest rate. The amount of available cash can vary greatly from one lender to the next.

- How will the cash be paid?—Depending on the lender, the cash from a reverse mortgage is typically available to the borrower in one of three ways. In some cases, a combination of payment methods may be available:
- Lump sum—the loan proceeds can be paid with one check, usually at the time the loan is closed.
- Periodic advances—cash payments of a fixed amount, usually monthly. Term advances are made for a specified period of time; tenure advances continue as long as the borrower lives in the home; lifetime advances are paid as long as the borrower lives.
- Credit line—a line of credit, the borrower can use when needed, up to the loan limit. Some credit lines are "Flat," i.e., the total amount of available credit is fixed. Other credit lines "Grow" and provides an amount of credit, which increases over time.
- Cost of the loan—Federal law requires reverse mortgage lenders to provide prospective borrowers with a loan cost analysis. The total annual loan cost (TALC) analysis looks at the cost of a loan under a specified set of circumstances, over the entire length of the loan. The standardized nature of the TALC makes it easy to compare the cost of loans from different lenders.
- Remaining equity—if a borrower decides to sell the home after only a few years, how much equity would be left?

MAJOR REVERSE MORTGAGE PROGRAMS

While there are a number of lenders in the private sector who make reverse mortgage loans, the two most widely available programs are operated under the auspices of the federal government:

- Federal Housing Administration (FHA)—the Federal Housing Administration, part of the U.S. Department of Housing and Urban development, insures reverse mortgage loans made by private lenders under its Home Equity Conversion Mortgage (HECM) program.

If a lender fails to make the promised payments, the FHA takes over responsibility for fulfilling the lender's obligations. The HECM program has specific loan limits and is targeted at moderate-income families.

- Federal National Mortgage Association (FNMA)—the Federal National Mortgage Association, also known as Fannie Mae is a government-created private corporation. FNMA operates the Home-Keeper-reverse mortgage program, with many features similar to the FHA's HECM program.

Additional Resources

The federal government entities directly involved with reverse mortgages, the FHA and FNMA, have freely available information on the details of each reverse mortgage program. Further, these agencies require consumer education as a part of the lending process. There are also several independent, third party sources of information on reverse mortgages:

- National Center for Home Equity Conversion (NCHEC)—the NCHEC is an independent, not-for-profit organization whose goal is to provide consumer education about home equity conversion options. On the Internet, their Web site is: *http://www.reverse.org*
- U.S. Department of Housing and Urban Development (HUD)—provides information on reverse mortgages, which is available from the U. S. Department of Housing and Urban Development at their Web site at: *http://www.hud.gov*

Seek Professional Advice

Because they are relatively new, reverse mortgages are unfamiliar to many. Also, those most likely to consider a reverse mortgage are usually at a point in life where long-term commitments must be very carefully considered. Individuals considering a reverse mortgage are strongly advised to seek professional advice before entering into a loan contract. All the implications must be weighed. As you have learned earlier, in other areas, do not seek the advice of a reverse mortgage specialist because they have a vested interest in providing the loan whether you need it or not. See a reverse mortgage specialist *after* you have made the decision, because they will have better knowledge of this unique product than most mortgage brokers.[22]

OK, I know what you are thinking: I still need to live somewhere! My point is not that you should not have a mortgage, but that you should minimize it and pay it off as soon as possible and do not get duped into believing that housing prices will never go down. People thought I was crazy for saying this, but now I look smart. It is funny how principles may seem to be suspended, but eventually they are proven to be true, just like gravity!

Cash Flow is Critical to Success

Once your major debts are out of the way, you can think about your personal cash management realistically. Now your liabilities are limited to true, monthly expenses rather than the effects of borrowing. In retirement, cash is king—is replaced by—cash flow is king.

Cash flow is essentially having cash in your wallet or account to do what you need or want at the moment of spending. You can have a great paycheck and little debt, but on a given day when your account only has $5 and there is nothing in your wallet, that is a bad cash flow day. You can also manage your cash so that you always have available, liquid cash any day of the month and that is good cash flow management. Cash flow is an entirely different concept from budgeting or spending, but it is directly affected and impacted by those activities. It's through money management that you can obtain good cash flow.

Paula Deen, a Food Network icon, has a lot of recipes that include the "House Seasoning." Emeril Lagasse's frequently used "Essence" and would "BAM!" them onto his dishes before serving. At some point in their careers, both these personalities assumed you knew what "House seasoning" and "Essence" were because it is an integral part of so many of their dishes and show, it was assumed that the audience knew what these were. The "House seasoning" and "Essence" in my cookbook is cash flow. It is the spice blend that is the foundation of so many decisions. Many problems can be avoided just by deciding if the decision has a negative or positive effect on cash flow.

Debt would be smaller, spending would be reduced, lifestyles would soar, and peace of mind would be attainable. Life would taste better! Just because we discuss cash flow overtly now, do not think that it has not seasoned this whole book.

INFLOW VS. OUTFLOW

A key concept in money management is managing your financial inflow versus outflow. Essentially inflow is all the money you receive or generate while outflow is all the money you spend. There is nothing subjective about these terms. Each should have a concrete and tangible number attached to it and you should know what that number is on a monthly basis and a yearly basis at the very least. The difference between the two is the amount of debt you are incurring or the amount of savings you are generating.[23]

Take the time to calculate what these two numbers are for your financial situation. We discussed this earlier however, be aware that most people tend to overestimate, underestimate or somehow leave off entire expenses when doing this exercise. If you use faulty input, you will get faulty output (garbage in, garbage out). Therefore, you need to be thorough when reviewing your expenses and income and take into consideration the things that often go unnoticed such as taxes, vacation money, educational needs, and medical expenses. If you use a software program for personal finance tracking then you will be one step ahead of the game and should already have these numbers available without calculating them yourself. But any tracking is a house of cards. If you don't keep up with regularly inputting your financial information, even the financial software reports won't mean anything to you.

Some people also like to include such things as the increase or decrease in value of tangible assets such as a house or vacation property. This can be included in the total assets, but keep in mind that the liquidity of physical property makes it impossible to include in cash flow analysis. Common physical assets that are often discussed as investments range from precious metals and houses all the way to baseball card collections. I usually discourage the use of these figures, however, because it is not most people's intentions to live on these. If you aren't going to live on the asset, then you should not include it.

Finally calculate the difference between these two numbers and see whether you have a positive or negative cash flow. What you are doing is taking the net income from all sources (including appreciation in value) and subtracting it from the net outflow (including net depreciation). This is probably the most important number in regards to your financial portfolio.

If on the other hand you have a negative number leftover, then you need to be aware that you are accumulating debt on a regular basis or dipping into your nest egg and are going to be eroding your principle in your retirement years. This *may* call for alarm. Most think that using the principle of your nest egg is wrong and that becomes the focus of their goal, which then causes much consternation when it does happen. If you are properly managing cash flow, you are pointed firmly toward your noble purpose, then depending on how quickly you are tapping your nest egg, and how old you are, will determine if there is cause for alarm. If you have followed the advice up to this point, you can relax. If you really want to breathe a sigh of relief, read on!

Rule #2: Lower Your Costs

One of the important aspects of obtaining your goals is to understand the costs of investing and the tax consequences of your investment decisions. Most people focus on the illusion of control, by trying to control the uncontrollable. They try to pick the perfect stock or try to time the market just right. Most gamblers believe that pulling the handle on a slot machine will give them a better chance at winning than pressing the button. Pressing the spin button or yanking the handle has no bearing on the outcome of a spin. The handle is nothing more than a connection to the switch that operates the spin button. But, many illusions are more powerful than reality. Gravity is an unseen reality, where flying is a visual illusion that appears to be violating that invisible reality. The unseen reality of the costs of investing and the tax consequences of your investment decisions can have a profound impact on your success.

Investing Costs

The next area to understand is that, just selling an investment at the wrong price is not the total loss. You also have other costs involved getting into and out of the market. To truly understand the full net value of what your market activity is, you also need to add in these expenses.

Cost is what you paid for a property, whether a stock or a bond, a mutual fund or a home—basis is the amount used for figuring any gain or loss when that property is sold. To calculate basis, certain adjustments are added to or subtracted from your cost.[24]

Costs of investing are any fees incurred by investors to buy, sell, and own stocks or mutual funds. What you don't see is hurting you. Think of what you consider too high of a cost to pay for a mutual fund, think of the number you think you are paying at one of the huge "Low cost" firms. Add 2 percent, and you are getting close to the real costs.

There are two main categories, explicit and implicit costs.

Explicit costs:

- Commissions—these mainly include brokerage commissions, but also include miscellaneous tasks, for which there are explicit accounting charges.
- Bid/Ask Spreads—the quoted spread between a bid price and ask price is the market maker's compensation for providing liquidity, analogous to the broker's commission. The bid-ask price varies depending on the stock's liquidity.

Implicit costs:

- Market Impact—the actual market-value-swing of the stock between target and purchase. Institutions make large trades and demand increasing liquidity from markets. As a result, their trades often move prices in the direction of the trade, resulting "Market impact" or "Price impact."
- Delay occurs when orders are on the buy side of the trade desk, but has not been released to the broker because the trader fears he may swamp the market.
- Missed trades—the natural consequence of the release delays: if the price moves too much before the trade can be completed, the manager will pull back on the trade.

Explicit plus Implicit = your total trading cost

Costs on Stocks

Bid/Ask spread has to do with how stocks are traded in the real world. If I get on the phone and called a major wirehouse right now, and say "I want to buy one hundred shares of (any large company) stock." The person on the other end might say, "You can buy that stock for $50 a share. And my commission is $25." Then if I turn around and say, "Wait a minute. I don't want to buy, I'm sorry, I want to sell one hundred shares" . . . I'm not going to be able to sell them for the same fifty they just quoted me. I might only be able to sell it for $49.50. Now, where does the difference between what I can buy for and what I can sell for, go? Well, I know you've seen all these guys running around the floor of the exchange with those little tickets on commercials, etc. Those guys are called market makers and specialists. You might think that I get to sell my shares of stock directly to you, but that isn't quite how it works. I have to sell my shares to the person on the floor of the exchange, which in effect works for the large brokerage firms. They take a profit off the top, and they turn around and sell it to the next investor. So every time a stock changes hands, they are taking a profit that goes to the brokerage houses or wirehouse that controls those markets. Whether you are an individual investor, or whether you are a big mutual fund, you're still paying the bid/ask spread costs.

First, let's define what a basis point is. A basis point is one hundredth of a percentage point (0.01 percent). Basis points are often used to measure changes in or differences between yields on fixed income securities, since these often change by very small amounts.[25]

In large stocks, such as those in the S&P or Fortune 500 companies, the bid/spread cost runs about 3 basis points (bp). So, if we want to do what we call a round trip, sell out of one stock and buy another, that is 3bp to sell, 3bp to buy, plus approximately 0.5 percent in commissions—that is about 0.56 percent.

A medium-sized company can easily run up to 11bp. So a round trip is about 11bp to sell and 11bp to buy—that's 0.22 percent plus commissions, which totals about 0.75 percent.

Now, have you ever seen one of those commercials on TV or the radio, where they say they won't charge you any commissions at all? How do they do that? Usually, those offers are exclusively for very, very small companies. The spread on a small company is easily 2.40 percent.

The 2.40 percent to sell, plus 2.40 percent to buy, that's 4.80 percent—well, thank you for not charging me a commission! It is so important to understand how that works. These big brokerage companies don't buy advertising spots during the Super Bowl off little commissions. They do this from "Making markets," that is how they make the money. This is just the beginning; it gets worse! It is no difference when you buy and sell a house. If I sell a house for $100,000, the buyer may pay $100,000, but I will not get a check for $100,000. Fees need to be paid! The financial markets are no different, except that the buyer and seller pay, and it is not as transparent as real estate transactions.

MUTUAL FUND FEES

The cost to the consumer of no-load mutual funds boils down to "What you can't see, *can* hurt you." This is right out of Charles Ellis's book, *How to Win the Loser's Game.* He says, "The key question under the new rules of the game is this: how much better must an actively trading manager be to at least recover the cost of the portfolio turnover? The answer is daunting. Total transaction costs, which are commissions plus the spread between the bid and the ask side of the market of 2 percent to buy and 2 percent to sell are certainly not high estimates."

In no-load mutual funds the total expense ratio average is 1.19 percent. Now add trading and bid/ask costs, which are a huge 4.17 percent average, and when you add it all up it can easily cost 5.36 percent of your investment money, inside of a so-called "No-load" mutual fund. "No-load" mutual funds are not load-free as you might expect.

Equity and bond funds are subject to capital gains, although fixed-income securities tend to generate smaller distributions. Short-term capital gains, on investments held less than a year, can be taxed at a rate of as much as low as 15 percent, but as high as 35 percent depending on the state you live in. Long-term gains on investments owned more than a year, have a 15 percent tax rate. Funds also pass through dividends and interest, paid by stocks and bonds they own. Municipal bond funds are the exception from federal taxes, and in some cases, state taxes. The only way to effectively avoid these taxes is to sell the fund holdings before the distribution date near the end of the calendar year, or to hold the funds in a 401(k) or IRA. So for every dollar you know, you spend on fund costs, another forty-three cents is spent on hidden costs. In the case of a high turnover, smaller funds, hidden costs can be as much as five to six times the expense ratio.[26]

So, in general, what you can't see, can even hurt you. Most fees and expenses are hidden from you; nevertheless, they can suck the returns right out of your portfolio. Better to pay a slightly higher disclosed fee than a huge hidden one. By far, the biggest costs for most investors are hidden trading costs.

In the excellent documentary, *Navigating the Fog of Investing*, Steve Wynn the casino/gambling magnate, is quoted as saying that the casino makes twenty cents on every dollar bet. The house is not concerned with who wins or loses it just needs people betting.

As long as you are trading, the brokerage firm is winning. To most brokerage firms, it doesn't matter if you make money or not. As long as you trade, they earn commissions, and many times the juicy and highly profitable bid/ask spreads. Up or down, they win. I think if Steve Wynn knew the numbers in the financial world, he would think he was underpaid.

It's not what you make, but what you keep, that counts. Portfolio turnover, or how often a manager buys and sells stock in your portfolio, can dramatically reduce your return in two ways. The first is internal market and trading costs. The second is by creating a huge tax bill.

I have a client that came to me for tax preparation when he had already been to two Certified Public Accountants, and several "Advisors" and none knew why his million-dollar portfolio in one of the world's largest mutual funds, had a $150,000 capital gain despite the fact that he started the year with one million and ended the year with one million and he had not sold the fund and he did not take any money out. The answer was simple, internal trades created capital gains (and profits for the fund). The following year was worse. He had capital gains and the corresponding taxes on the same fund that went down. That is when he became a client.

The famous John Bogle, founder of Vanguard Funds, has this to say, "Most investors in stocks think they can avoid the pitfalls of investing by due diligence and knowledge, trading stocks with alacrity to stay one step ahead of the game. But while the investors who trade the least have a fighting chance of capturing the market's return, those who trade the most are doomed to failure." [27]

John Bogle continues, "Mutual fund investors, too, have inflated ideas of their own omniscience. They pick funds based on the recent performance superiority of fund managers, or even their long-term superiority, and hire advisers to help them do the same thing. But, the advisers do it with even less success. Oblivious of the toll taken by costs, fund investors willingly pay heavy sales loads and incur excessive fund fees and expenses, and are unknowingly subjected to the substantial, but hidden transaction costs incurred by funds as a result of their hyperactive portfolio turnover. Fund investors are confident that they can easily select superior fund managers. They are wrong."[28]

He, who trades less, wins. A broker's job is to get you to buy and sell as much as possible. Whether it is stocks, ETFs, mutual funds, or variable annuities—that is the primary way he or she gets paid. This is a huge conflict of interest because what is good for you is bad for the broker. The difference is what a managed mutual fund is worth with all of its trading versus the raw behavior of the S&P 500.

Had enough of the fees? There are still more! If you got your mutual fund from a broker/dealer, then you have a whole other set of fees. Some other fees to watch out for, in mutual funds:

- No-Load—no salesman commission.
- Shares—salesman gets paid a commission upfront, plus a trail.
- B Shares—no upfront sales charge, but additional fees and a fee on the way out if you sell it "Too soon"
- C Shares—1 percent annual fee forever
- D Shares—1 percent front-end load and additional annual fees of at least .50 percent

Had enough fees yet? Add to all that we have discussed, another couple of fees, if you were to choose to own your mutual funds inside a variable annuity. Typically, you will add mortality expense, aka M/E expense, of 1.5 percent and then add the income rider of typically .6 percent. This adds to your recipe for disaster. If you have been wondering why you can't get ahead, now you know. It is fees!

In my opinion, the variable annuity is the worst product ever offered to the public. In Suze Orman's *The Road to Wealth*, she sums up my sentiments in an answer to a question on page 504. "My financial adviser is recommending that I buy a variable annuity within my retirement account. What should I do? Get yourself another financial adviser, pronto." She should have added an exclamation point.

Since I have digressed into the world of annuities, let's deal with them more clinically and for that, I will turn it over to syndicated radio host, Peter D'Arruda.

Key Considerations of Variable Annuities[29]

Tax Issues

Your gains are not taxed until you take the money out, which is good news. However, the downside is that when you do pay, it is at regular income tax rates. If you held comparable investments in a mutual fund, for example, you would pay much lower capital gain tax rates.

Early Withdrawal Penalties

Variable annuities have low flexibility because they are intended for retirement savings. Investors will have to pay surrender fees if he or she needs to withdraw money from the variable annuity within a set period following its purchase. Typically, if you need to withdraw more than 10 percent of your money in the first few years, the variable annuities' surrender charge will be a percentage of the amount withdrawn in the range of 5 to 10 percent and scaling down each year, eventually to 0 percent over the course of the next six to ten years.

Before investing, be sure you will be leaving the investment intact for a minimum of ten years. Studies have shown than an investor needs to own a variable annuity for ten to twenty years for the investment to make sense from a fee and financial common sense standpoint.

Death Benefit

If you have to die to get your money back, do you really have acceptable investment protection?

Variable annuities include a death benefit that will provide your heirs with at least the total amount you invested—even if your account has lost money—if you die before the annuity payments begin. This may sound good, but there is a fee associated with this feature. It is an option you can purchase. However, this is essentially a life insurance policy within your variable annuity, but the cost of this insurance is five to ten times greater than the cost of life insurance you could purchase on your own.

Living Benefit

Many variable annuities salespeople are boosting sales by pushing "Life benefits." They sell this benefit saying you can get back your entire investment, even if you have had a loss, if you withdraw the money during retirement years. However, what actually happens is that the company will pay you a yearly payment, but the company maintains control of your investment. In addition, investors have to pay a fee to purchase this option.

Churning and Excessive Fees

The unnecessary replacement of an old variable annuity with a new variable annuity creates unnecessary commission to the broker and brand new surrender fees to the client.

False Disclosures

Many times, variable annuity brokers fail to disclose investment risks or misrepresent benefits that can be achieved through variable annuities. Potential investors should ask for everything in writing and then thoroughly examine the prospectus before investing. (A magnifying glass is recommended.)

Request the broker to put all the charges in writing and give you a signed statement disclosing the total fees, charges, expenses, and commissions.

Fees and Costs

Variable annuities, with a death benefit, usually cost 50-100 percent more in annual fees than comparable investments. Likewise, life benefits add 20 percent or more per year to the cost of variable annuities. Many variable annuities also have annual fees in their sub-accounts, which add to the investor's cost. In addition, annual fees, surrender fees, and early withdrawal penalties have contributed to variable annuities' relatively high fees when compared to other investment options.

Getting Out

If you are trapped in a poor-performing variable annuity, or you are tired of paying all the fees, commissions, and expenses, there are other alternatives. You may be able to transfer your money directly to another annuity company without paying taxes through a vehicle known as a 1035 tax-free exchange. There still may be some surrender charges, so make sure you understand the costs associated with such an exchange.

Recommended Types of Annuities

Unlike variable annuities, the following types of annuities may be a wise addition to an investment portfolio: Fixed, Immediate, and Indexed.

Fixed

Fixed annuities operate similar to CDs purchased at the bank. An insurance company guarantees—for a set period of time—a periodic, set payment, and a minimum interest rate. Make sure to determine whether the rate is guaranteed or adjustable.

Immediate

Immediate annuities act like an individual pension plan. They guarantee an income for life—no matter how long you live, which is useful in connection with estate planning and life insurance. Some immediate annuities offer payment to a beneficiary following your death, while others waive beneficiary payments in exchange for a larger income stream while you are still alive. Immediate annuities are typically purchased with a one-time, lump-sum payment and are ideal for those who are retired or very near retirement age. They offer immediate return on investment, a steady stream of income for the rest of one's life, and underlying piece of mind. The income payments you receive, supplement your other sources such as Social Security or pension plans.

Fixed Indexed

Fixed Indexed Annuities are very popular in the market because they protect investment dollars while offering a share of the market upside without downside risk. They combine features of traditional insurance products with traditional securities and are ideal for investors who want the potential for higher returns, combined with a guarantee. The insurance company pays a rate of return to the Fixed Indexed Annuity investor that is based on the changes to an equity index such as the S&P 500. Therefore, the investor benefits when stock prices rise, but does not lose money if prices go down. A minimum return is usually guaranteed.

It is important to understand what the upside limits are, and how interest is computed. There are many different Fixed Indexed Annuities available, with varying terms from one to twenty plus years. Make sure to get the one that is appropriate for your situation. For more information, contact a professional that specializes in Annuity Planning.[30]

UNDERSTAND THE GOAL OF FINANCIAL SERVICES

Financial Services cover a lot ground. They can involve brokerages, banks, advisors, insurance companies, even nonprofit organizations and, believe it or not, church organizations. So who are some of the more common players? Let's look.

First, what is a broker? Many of you who are reading this work with a broker, of course, their names are disguised as registered representatives. Maybe you are working with the Executive Vice President of Domestic and Global Acquisitions. You are working with a broker. A broker is a person who makes money when you buy something, and he makes money when you sell something. A broker makes money when you make money and the broker makes money when you lose money. It's the ultimate middle-man business—a broker is somebody who is transaction-oriented. Most brokers work directly for or with a Broker/Dealer who also gets part of and facilitates the Broker transactions.

A banker is essentially a representative of a bank. Today's banks are mainly corporations with divisions in all sorts of financial activities, so the term "banker" is not as synonymous with the local neighborhood bank, as it is with specific corporations known to be banking institutions. Think Bank of America, Citigroup, Chase, or Wells Fargo, those are technically banks, but also corporations. Their managers and representatives are, in essence, bankers.

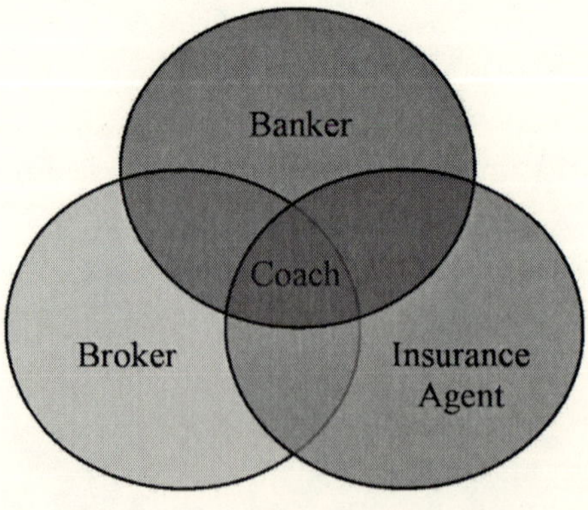

An *insurance agent* is a representative of an insurance company. Whether it is State Farm, AAA, Nationwide, or Allstate, every insurance company has agents. That's because the term "agent" means more than just a sales representative (even though the majority of their work is sales of insurance policies), it also gives them authority to represent their companies on existing policies with existing customers. When you have a claim or you want to make a policy change, you deal with an agent. Underwriters in the home office actually make decisions, but the agent is the person who negotiates with you for the insurance company. The insurance company pays them on all the policies they sell, where they are getting paid indirectly by one of the policies you own. A subtle, but substantial distinction that is compounded if the agent is "Captive," meaning they sell exclusively what Allstate says they can sell.

A financial strategist and coach is a professional who helps people deal with various personal financial issues through proper planning, which includes, but is not limited to these major areas: cash flow management, education planning, retirement planning, investment planning, risk management and insurance planning, tax planning, estate planning, and business succession planning (for business owners). The work, engaged in by these professionals, is commonly known as personal financial planning. In carrying out the planning function, he is guided by the financial planning process to create a financial plan; a detailed strategy tailored to a client's specific situation, for meeting a client's specific goals. It's like a business plan, but for an individual's needs rather than a business.

A banker can sell you CDs and bank accounts and may sideline as a broker and sell you stocks and mutual funds. A broker can do the same, but mostly won't have access to bank account services. An insurance agent can sell you life insurance, casualty insurance, and annuities, but not market instruments, well, at least, most of the time, some can.

Are you confused? You are not alone.

In 2006, TD Ameritrade Institutional found in a survey that 54 percent of investors believed both brokers and independent registered investment advisors (RIAs) have a responsibility to act in their best interests. They found that 74 percent of investors did not understand the different obligations required of RIAs and brokers.

Did you know that RIAs have an obligation to act in investors' best interests in all aspects of the financial relationship? RIAs have a fiduciary duty a broker has only to meet suitability standards.

Investment advisors provide their clients with a Form ADV that describes exactly who the investment advisor does business with, how they do it, how they are compensated, in other words there is full disclosure well before recommendations are made. For example, this book is on my ADV.

Investment advisors do not engage in business activities like investment banking or underwriting, which brokerage firms do. No RIA firms received TARP funds or were acquired in an emergency "shotgun wedding" during the 2008 financial meltdown.

All of the above quickly gets to the core question—what should an investor expect from their advisor? Many investors actually want advice, but don't necessarily know how to communicate that correctly or apply it to their market choices.[31] Most don't even know what to look for or who to start with?

Allow me to create an analogy that will show you how to pick an advisor. Imagine you walked into a home improvement center and tracked down a person in the colored apron. You told them you were going to BBQ and needed help. They would likely point you in the direction of the grills and grilling accessories. Now walk into a grocery store and ask for help with your BBQ. You are likely to be pointed to the cold section in the back full of meat. Now why is it that you asked for the same thing at two stores and got two different answers? Not a tough riddle, they are two very different retail stores with two completely different sets of inventory.

Let's make it a little more difficult. What if I was risk averse and needed investment advice and I walked into a bank and asked for help with advice on what to do to protect the principle on my money. You should know the answer you are going to get from the bank. They will recommend a certificate of deposit, aka CD. What if you were to contact an insurance agent for advice? They would recommend an annuity. If you contacted a broker with the same risk aversion they would likely recommend a highly rated municipal bond. See the problem? You asked for the same "Advice" from three financial advisors and got three different options. Which one is right? The answer is simple, but the solution is far more complex. It depends on your other goals, your tax bracket, your liquidity needs, how much you are looking to invest and what objectives you have other than, preserve principle. Also, what exactly is this money for? Answers to all these questions and more will affect the answer.

In the BBQ example, you knew you were walking into different stores, therefore you would get different advice. Before this example, most of you did not realize that when getting financial advice, you were getting it from a retail outlet that only has inventory limited to what that store carries. So you weren't getting advice, you were getting sold. I am not knocking sales. It is the world's oldest profession (I know what you are thinking, but you are focusing on the product being sold). I am an ethical free-market capitalist, so I believe in sales. The world revolves around the movement of products and services. The problem is that the process is backward.

In broadly based planning, that our complicated lives and tax code force us to deal with, we need advice first, products second. This equation points out that products have their place, which is last!

Values, Vision, Goals

Strategies, Tactics, Products

The temptation at this point is to personally manage your financial portfolios, to do it yourself, and avoid the mess. You can do it yourself with your own research, you can pay monthly fees to Web sites that provide you collected sources that you browse through yourself, and you can make managing your assets, your full-time job in retirement. The problem with this is that you are still limited in your access to products and this will be very, very important. (I will cover this in detail in rule 3). That is why you are looking for a financial strategist *and* coach. Here are some thoughts about professional financial advice:[32]

> **Strategy and planning is more than investing.** Not all planners offer comprehensive services. Some just give investment advice or focus on one aspect of planning, such as insurance or taxes. You need someone that sees the taxes, insurance, and financial aspects and have no interest in anything other than making sure that you win in all those areas and at the same time understand where and how the three connect.
>
> **Is it a match?** When hiring a strategist and coach, find the one that can deliver the services you need and who's compatible with your style and your philosophies. Also, make sure you like them!
>
> **Personal references are a good place to start.** A reference from a friend or family member is a great way to start a search. But make sure you've got similar needs as the person who's giving the referral. If you do not like French food, you would not go to a restaurant, a friend recommended that was French no matter how great the recommendation.
>
> **Understand how your planner is getting paid.** The three most common setups are:

- Fee-only-Fee-*only* planners don't get commissions for the products they sell-fees are for the advice they give.

Pro: All fees—appearance of no conflict of interest.
Con: There are some great products that only pay commissions. If handled correctly that commission products can lower fees.

- Fee-based-Fee-*based* planners may receive commission on some products they sell, but most of their money comes from a fee you pay them.

Pro: Have access to most of the products.
Con: Can be tilted heavily to commissions.

- Commission-based—Commission-based planners are paid by the companies whose products they sell.

Pro: Appears to be free.
Con: Far more expensive in the long run. Conflict of interest.

Check credentials. Check to see if a planner's record is tarnished by disciplinary problems or complaints. Groups that award credentials or state agencies keep tabs on planners and can provide help.

Express yourself. The quality of a planner's advice is correlated to how well he or she knows you. Make sure a planner asks questions about your finances, goals, risk tolerance, and philosophy. If they don't ask, they probably aren't paying adequate attention, or they don't care because they are going to stick you in the same product as everyone else that comes in to your office.

Know what they're selling. Find out what financial products a planner sells and how much he or his firm earns for making a sale. Be wary of planners who push one product, say, one family of mutual funds or one kind of insurance, as they are not giving you the unbiased or comprehensive advice you need.

Know yourself. The best planner will take his cues from you. Before you hire someone, identify the financial goals you want to meet, your assets and liabilities, your risk tolerance, and investment style.

Know their licenses. This may be the most important piece of information you can get. How they are licensed will tell you how they can get compensated. How they are compensated will tell you how they give advice. In my research I have determined the perfect fit to be someone with an insurance license and a Series sixty-five, securities license. This licensing-set-limits commissions to the insurance world and minimizes expenses on the securities side.

However, you need to remember that financial advisors are in the business to make a profit. As a result, just like any field where practitioners have built-in conflict of interest competing with your best interests, there are bad financial advisors too. Five signs of a bad financial advisor include:

- *You own a mutual fund with the letter "A, B, or C" in its name.* These funds are "Loaded" funds as explained earlier. These funds are known as deferred-sales charge funds: If you cash out in the first year, you'll pay a commission of, say, 5 percent of the money you pull out; if you leave in the second year, the fee is 4 percent, and so on. After five years or so, you typically won't pay a fee when you sell. But the longer you stay invested in the fund, the longer you'll be paying a very steep expense ratio. That's the annual charge all mutual fund investors pay on their investment. The problem with B share funds is that the expense ratio can be 1.5 percent a year or more, because a big portion of that charge goes to pay the advisor who sold you the fund. When you compare that to index funds or exchange-traded funds (ETFs), which have expense ratios that can be just two-tenths of a percentage point or less (0.20 percent), it's a huge difference. Your advisor is doing well, but the high expense ratio you're paying makes it harder for you to do well.[33] The licenses the advisor would need to carry these products are the Series 6 and 63 or 7.

- *You pay the advisor through commissions only.* A financial advisor—who can just be a gussied-up name for broker—who makes all of his or her money on commissions from the investments you buy and sell obviously has an interest in getting you to do a lot of buying and selling. And it's not unreasonable to see that the advisor has a financial incentive to get you to pay high commissions. A typical advisor fee might be 1 percent to 1.5 percent or so. But again, you need to be careful that your advisor is taking good care of your money. If you're paying an advisor 1 percent or so a year for his fee, and the advisor is then turning around and putting you in mutual funds with annual expense ratios of around 1.5 percent, your total investing costs are way too high. A financial advisor who charges a flat annual management fee should be focused on individual stocks or very low-cost funds such as index funds, market funds, or ETFs. [34]
- *Your life insurance is a cash-value policy.* If your advisor also happens to be a life insurance agent and has steered you into a cash-value policy, sirens

should be blaring in your head. In the vast majority of cases, all you need is a simple-term insurance policy, which is going to cost you about 80 percent less than a cash-value policy as an investment (rules are different for estate planning) such as universal life, whole life, or variable life. Why would someone recommend an expensive cash-value policy? Well, one strong possibility is that the agent's commission is a percentage of your premium, and the higher cash-value premium translates into a larger commission for the agent.[35]

- *You own a variable annuity.* The spin on variable annuities is that you get tax-deferred growth in mutual funds-that is, no taxes while the money is invested in the VA. But in truth, everything in your IRA is already tax-deferred anyway! Additional spin might include, you get stock market returns, but your principle is protected. I can easily deconstruct why this is on its face is true, but when you follow the "Rules" of the Variable Annuity game, you will *have* to do things that will give you an outcome you are not happy with. Plenty has been written on just how bad these products are, but the big commissions and the great trails make the sale of this product is too hard to resist. To prove how bad variable annuities are, I call the product company with the annuity owner in my office, on a speaker phone. I then ask direct questions about how the product "Really" works and virtually every client I have done this with asks how to get out of the product after we have hung up the phone. Even after disclosing the losses from surrender charges they want out. You should too.
- *You're saving for your kid's college education rather than your retirement.* One reason many people turn to financial advisors is for help in figuring out how to save money for their children's college educations. While it's logical to want to provide for your kids, a good financial advisor won't blindly set up college

> funds for you. Instead, a good financial advisor will assess whether you should be saving for college at all. If you aren't already maxing out on all your own retirement savings options, or you have a big chunk of high-interest credit card debt, you have no business putting your kid's college costs ahead of getting your own finances in good shape. A financial advisor who has your best interests at heart, and your kid's for that matter, will explain that if you retire without sufficient income to live on, or in serious debt, you're going to be a financial burden to your child no matter how good his/her college education is.

The use of multiple financial advisors is a widespread, if rarely publicized, aspect of today's investment landscape, particularly among people in the mass affluent investment bracket—a term used to describe folks with investable assets of between $500,000 and $3 million. Portfolios of that size begin to require more complicated plans, strategies, and long-term goals, which often prompt investors to look beyond the services of one advisor. There are good reasons to be less-than-exclusive when seeking investment advice and services: The right mix can help your investments and get the most out of what you pay for. But there are also bad reasons for using multiple advisors and the bad in this case far outweigh the good. The worst is an inclination to secrecy and resistance in disclosing your full array of assets to any one advisor. This leads to bad planning, which makes it more difficult to reach goals. It is like running with ankle weights on; you'll get there, but not as fast. Also a single source provider can cut your costs, reduce tax hassles, and ward off unnecessary damage to your portfolio. If you follow the advice I have outlined, there is no need for multiple advisors, just one good one. The final step addresses the business side of the advisor's business. If you understand how they are structured, you will understand what kind of advice you are getting and why.

FOUR DIFFERENT BUSINESS MODELS USED

Another misunderstood part of the investment landscape is the whole business of financial/investment advisors. The product angle we talked about above is one component, but it is still far more complex than that. Once you know the above facts, how do you know who exactly to turn to? Here are the most common business models used in the marketplace today:

The "horizontal rectangle" all-in-one type of a financial planning business is a smorgasbord of services. The advisor basically tries to offer everything. Have you ever had one of those Boy Scout camping knives that were loaded with every gizmo imaginable? At first it's pretty amazing what's included. But guess what? You don't need 90 percent of the junk on that all-in-one tool. In fact, so much attention has been put into trying to have every possibility, that the quality of the individual tools included is inferior. It's the same with services using a rectangle model. They try to cast the widest net so that they have every possibility a customer can want, but they have very little expertise in any of the offerings. Think of the general practitioner in the medical field. Everyone needs the family doctor, and it is a great starting point, but at some point you will need a specialist. If you have a heart problem, your family doctor is just not going to cut it; pun intended. This is the "Expert at many, master at none" approach. Stay away from advisors that have adopted this model.

The "vertical rectangle," this second model is similar to the first, except that the rectangle is vertical instead of horizontal. This is a very narrow and very specific model. This model goes after a very specific target market and sells them a specific product. The best example of this from the financial services industry is a person selling a 403(b) to the teacher market. The 403(b) is a very specific product being sold to a very specific market. A medical analogy would be like the ENT or Ear Nose Throat doctor. But even more specific than an Ear Nose Throat doctor, would be just an ear doctor and to follow the analogy further, an ear doctor for only seniors. This is an excellent business model; it is highly specialized so the expertise is very high. Unfortunately, it is very difficult to find one such, in the financial services industry.

The inverted triangle (single point is down) is the most-pervasive approach. This sales model is very common, particularly for brokerages who already know what they want to sell. Every question that is asked and every answer is going to be bent back to selling what the brokerage wants to deal in, regardless. They will say they offer a diversity of investments and tools, but if their target product is separately managed accounts (SMAs), stock portfolios, mutual fund portfolios, or a singular product like a Fixed Indexed Annuity or a Variable Annuity, eventually everything you say you want, will come back to selling to you, what they want you to own—no matter what. It is like a funnel, everything goes into the top and it all comes out at one point. This is the model of most commission-based advisors and financial "Stores."

I would like to give you a medical analogy on this one, but there isn't one that even comes close. This shows just how self-serving and company-centric this model is. This model is the most-pervasive and is so bad that I have memorized (through repetition) the ticker symbols of some of the mutual funds that are *always* on a particular broker/dealer statements.

The final model is without question the best model. This model looks like a standard triangle, the point is up. This model has a singular market focus, like tax and retirement planning, college funding or business succession planning. It has a much wider product mix. So if my market was the baby boomer, and I focused only on retirement planning for the baby boomers, then I would carry every conceivable product that would serve this market segment. If a new product comes out, regardless of the sizzle, if it doesn't serve my market segment, then I wouldn't carry it. However, I would carry a wide range of products and services so that I can best serve my singular market without offering the same thing to everyone I met. This is also a very difficult model to find, but without question, the best. If it is so good, why don't more companies use it? Because, it is more difficult to build, implement, and manage.

Understanding these business models will help you pay lower fees in the long run.

INFLATION

Like many of the hidden fees already discussed, this is hidden as well. There are very few areas that can have a bigger impact on success or failure and so few people factor it into the planning process.

What is inflation? It's the increase in the cost of goods throughout our economy that will impact your purchasing power. This is a real issue in retirement due to many people being on fixed incomes in retirement. For example, starting with an annual income of $50,000 with 4 percent inflation annually, in eighteen years you will need $100,000 to maintain the same lifestyle.

In economics, inflation is a rise in the general level of prices of goods and services in an economy over a period of time. The term "Inflation" once referred to increases in the money supply (monetary inflation); however, economic debates about the relationship between money supply and price levels have led to its primary use today in describing price inflation. Inflation can also be described as a decline in the real value of money—a loss of purchasing power. When the general price level rises, each unit of currency buys fewer goods and services. A chief measure of price inflation is the inflation rate, which is the percentage change in a price index over time.

Inflation can cause adverse effects on the economy. For example, uncertainty about future inflation may discourage investment and saving. High inflation may lead to shortages of goods as consumers begin hoarding them out of concern, their prices will increase in the future.

The important point to take away from the topic of inflation is that your financial plan needs to have a cohesive strategy and outpace the effects of inflation. Think of it like rust on metal. Unaddressed, the metal eventually weakens and breaks, becoming useless. Your financial plan is that metal being attacked by rust. You need a constant maintenance to clean it up, so your need to plan on increasing your income by at least 3 percent a year to keep inflation at bay. This is what it has averaged for the last one hundred years! That said, with the recent nonstop printing of currency to deal with the economic meltdown in 2008, the inflation numbers are projected to jump dramatically in the coming years.

A common inflation hedge is gold. I can't emphasize enough how bad an investment gold is. Those that benefit from gold are those that buy and sell gold! Gold has very limited use. Aside from it being used in very limited industrial applications and jewelry, its only value is a speculative value. The only rise in gold is because of a change in feelings not a change in real value. It does not earn interest, it does not earn dividends, and it cannot use compounding because of this. You cannot walk into a grocery store and buy a loaf of bread with a bar of gold. We left the gold standard years ago. Still not convinced?

In the book *Stocks for the Long Run*, Jeremy Siegel has a graph that shows what would have happened to a single dollar invested in gold, bonds, and stocks since 1801.

One dollar invested in bonds in 1801 would yield $13,975 today.

One dollar invested in stocks in 1801 would be worth $8.8 million today.

One dollar invested in gold in 1801 would be worth $14 today.

Here is an example from a single lifetime of investing.

If you would have invested $100,000 in 1929 until 2008 directly into the Consumer Price Index (inflation measurement calculation) you would have $1,233,000. This is your "Return" at inflation rates. The same $100,000 would have grown to $1,860,000 in one month T-Bills, or CDs. The same $100,000 in Gold would have grown to $4,386,768. Now if you are a gold bug, you are excited, thinking I have made your point for you. Not so fast. A broadly diversified portfolio (more on this later) would have given you $378,344,000! A well-built portfolio is your best hedge against inflation. Your average return *above* inflation would have been 8.79 percent. If you still think gold is a great idea because you know a guy, or an uncle that cleaned up with gold, then build it into your portfolio using Rule 3 of Financial Gravity, but I still have not finished dealing with all of rule two.

TAXES

The famous American writer, Mark Twain, who based his stories on life in the American 1800s, once said that there were two things a person can know for sure:

- He will die
- He will be taxed

You pay taxes on everything as this poem eloquently states.

The Tax Poem

Tax his land,
Tax his wage,
Tax his bed, in which he lays.

Tax his tractor,
Tax his mule,
Teach him, tax is the rule.

Tax his cow,
Tax his goat,
Tax his pants,
Tax his coat.

Tax his ties,
Tax his shirts,
Tax his work,
Tax his dirt.

Tax his tobacco,
Tax his drink,
Tax him if he tries to think.

Tax his booze,
Tax his beers,
If he cries,
Tax his tears.

Tax his bills,
Tax his gas,
Tax his notes,
Tax his cash.

Tax him good and let him know,
That after taxes, he has no dough.

If he hollers,
Tax him more,
Tax him until he's good and sore.

Tax his coffin, Tax his grave,
Tax the sod, in which he lays.

Put these words upon his tomb,
"Taxes drove me to my doom!"

And when he's gone,
We won't relax,
We'll still be after the inheritance *tax* !!
(Author hid Identity to Avoid Taxes?)

The Tax-Hit Parade!

Accounts Receivable Tax
Building Permit Tax
CDL License Tax
Cigarette Tax
Corporate Income Tax
Dog License Tax
Federal Income Tax
Federal Unemployment Tax (FUTA)
Fishing License Tax
Food License Tax
Fuel Permit Tax
Gasoline Tax
Hunting License Tax
Inheritance Tax
Inventory Tax
IRS Interest Charges (tax on top of tax),
IRS Penalties (tax on top of tax),
Liquor Tax,
Luxury Tax,
Marriage License Tax,
Medicare Tax,
Property Tax,
Real Estate Tax,
Service charge taxes,
Social Security Tax,
Road Usage Tax (Truckers),
Sales Taxes,

Recreational Vehicle Tax,
School Tax,
State Income Tax,
State Unemployment Tax (SUTA),
Telephone Federal Excise Tax,
Telephone Federal Universal Service Fee Tax,
Telephone Federal, State, and Local Surcharge Tax,
Telephone Minimum Usage Surcharge Tax, Telephone Recurring and Nonrecurring Charges Tax,
Telephone State and Local Tax,
Telephone Usage Charge Tax,
Utility Tax,
Vehicle License Registration Tax,
Vehicle Sales Tax,
Watercraft Registration Tax,
Well Permit Tax,
Workers Compensation Tax.
Did I miss any?

According to the book, *The Two Income Trap*, by Elizabeth Warren and Amelia Tyagi, the average *single-income* family from the 1970s had more discretionary income (46 percent) than the average *two-income* family today (25 percent).

Want to take a wild guess what makes up most of the difference? Taxes. Taxes went from 24 percent of the average single-income family in the 1970s to 34 percent of an average two-income family today. Taxes have gone up more than mortgages, health care, car expenses . . . more than everything!

I know after reading this it becomes difficult to even function, let alone do complicated analysis. It is important in a discussion like this to make sure that we don't become as they say, penny-wise and dollar-foolish. Often people come into my office who have made decisions because they didn't want to pay taxes (like the mortgage discussion earlier). And that decision cost them far more money than the taxes would have cost. I, like you, hate taxes. I, like you, have to make decisions based on the tax code, but with this in mind, it is, once again very important that we make mathematical decisions, not emotional ones, and many times when it comes to taxes, people side on the emotional. For example, I had a client who lost a lot of money in a single stock, because they refused to sell the stock when I suggested because of the capital gains tax they would've paid. The 15 percent capital gains tax paled in comparison to the 30 percent, ninety-day loss. That and not letting the tax "Tail wag the dog."

Before we tackle taxes, there are some basic principles that should govern all decisions and discussions about taxes. This comes from Ron Blue, a CPA and owner of one the most successful tax and financial planning businesses in the country.[36]

1. There is a direct correlation between income and income taxes due.
2. Tax reduction is a legitimate goal.
3. Tax reduction should never be the "Tail that wags the dog." *Examples of tax shelters and mortgage deductions.*
4. Inability to pay taxes due is symptomatic of poor planning.
5. Tax reduction and debt reduction are in direct conflict with one another. *In order to decrease your taxes you must decrease your income, which decreases your ability to pay off debt.*
6. Ultimately, *all* income, from whatever source, is taxed.
7. Tax avoidance and tax evasion are two entirely different things.
8. There are no free tax deductions.
9. Disagreeing with the government is not a legitimate reason to not pay taxes.

FOUR TYPES OF TAXES

There are four main categories of taxes for the individual. The first is the most well-known by most readers.

Income Tax: Personal or an individual's income tax is levied, based on the total income of the individual (with some deductions permitted). It's often collected on a pay-as-you-earn basis, with small corrections made soon after the end of the tax year. These corrections take one of two forms: payments to the government, for taxpayers who have not paid enough during the tax year and tax refunds from the government for those who have overpaid. Income tax systems will often have deductions available that lessen the total tax liability by reducing total taxable income. They may allow losses from one type of income to be counted against another. For example, a loss on the stock market may be deducted against taxes paid on wages.

Payroll Tax: The second most common tax is the one that anyone employed has experienced on a regular basis. A payroll tax generally refers to two kinds of taxes. They are taxes which employers are required to withhold from employees' pay, also known as withholding, and pay-as-you-earn (PAYE) or pay-as-you-go (PAYG) tax. These withholdings contribute to repayment of an employee's personal income tax obligation; if the payments exceed this obligation, the employee may be eligible for a tax refund or carry forward to future periods.

The other group of payroll taxes is paid from the employer's own funds, either as a fixed charge per employee or as a percentage of each employee's pay. Payroll taxes often cover government social insurance programs such as social security, health care, unemployment, and disability. These payments do not count toward income taxes of employees and employers, but are normally deductible by the employers.

Many of you may have heard of the self-employment tax, but this is just the employer portion that has to be paid by the "Self," because they are their own employer. I have had the question asked, "Can I avoid the self-employment tax by incorporating?" Here is the definition from the IRS Web site, "Self-employment tax (SE tax) is a social security and Medicare tax primarily for individuals who work for themselves. It is similar to the social security and Medicare taxes withheld from the pay of most wage earners." The IRS calls it "Similar" I call it the same, but you can't avoid the tax, you can only change what it is called.

Capital Gains Tax: Once you invest, you will be introduced to a new tax category, the capital gains tax. A capital gain is the difference between what you paid for an investment and what was received when you sold that investment. Investments include mutual funds, bonds, stocks, options, precious metals, real estate, and collectibles. If you sold an investment for more than what you paid for it, then you have a gain. If you sold an investment for less than what you paid for it, then you have a capital loss. In many cases, the amount of a capital gain is treated as income and subject to the marginal rate of income tax. However, in an inflationary environment, capital gains may be to some extent illusory: if prices in general have doubled in five years, then selling an asset for twice the price it was purchased for five years earlier represents no gain at all. Partly to compensate for such changes in the value of money over time, the United States historically gives a favorable capital gains tax rate based on the length of holding. If I bought a stock that doubled in two years, that would be favorable. Of course, if the US were to cause the gains through monetary policy and then taxed the inflated asset—*favorable* would not be the right word, maybe I should say *less bad*?

You pay capital gains even if you lose your shirt investing. In 2008, investors in the $4 billion Templeton Foreign Fund lost more than 50 percent of their money and now will be forced to pay taxes on as much as $1 billion of gains from the sales of investments. Managers had to sell profitable holdings [in 2008] as customer redemptions increased, resulting in short-and long-term capital gains. The result, of course, means tax bills for investors in the worst year since the 1930s.[37]

That's salt on an open wound!

If this isn't bad enough, it gets worse. Mutual fund managers started to trade more frequently to offset the huge losses they were receiving over the course of 2008. They generated additional capital gains and fees from these trades, further eroding your assets.

Estate Tax: So after working your whole life and paying taxes on all the income that you have earned saving diligently and paying taxes on the investment returns that you've earned. Paying taxes all along the way on everything you spent in everything you did. If you've managed to accumulate wealth then you have the ultimate insult, which is the estate tax. This is the government saying that despite our best efforts to prevent you from succeeding, you clearly have succeeded. Congratulations, now we want half!

The inheritance tax, estate tax, and death duty are the names given to various taxes, which arise on the death of an individual.

Excise Tax?—OK, we said four categories, but there always is the potential for the government to go back on its word.

Today there is over $10 Trillion in retirement plans. Not too long ago in the 1990s, we had an "Excise" tax (15 percent) on retirement plans that were deemed to be too large. Could Congress bring the excise tax back? It's as easy as changing a law. The point here is that with all of the financial challenges facing our government, could they elect to reinstate an excise tax back on retirement plans. Anything is possible. It is not wise to plan for possibilities, but it is smart to plan for probabilities.

THE EGG CONCEPT

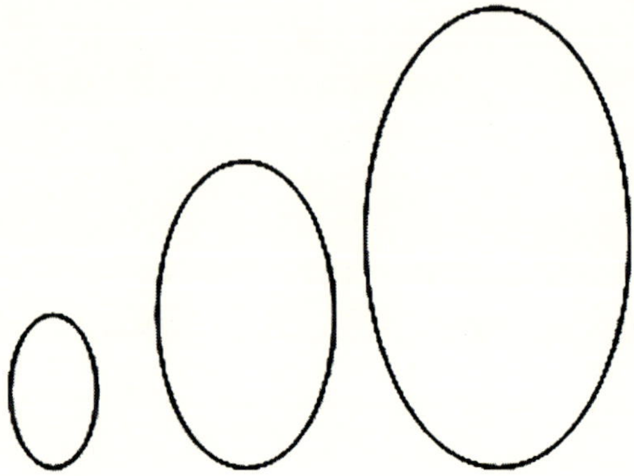

I realize what I'm about ready to discuss is an oversimplification of an exceptionally complex tax code. However, my goal is not to make you a tax attorney, it is to give you a working knowledge of the tax code so that you can make better decisions. The small egg represents the money you earn, the medium egg represents the money you grow, and a large egg represents the money you distribute at retirement, hopefully. There are various ways to avoid taxes within the three eggs.

Typically, we choose to avoid taxes on the first egg, our earnings, tax defer the second egg in something like a 401(k) and pay taxes on the third egg, when we distribute it at retirement. Basically, we choose to avoid taxes on the one hen and to pay taxes on all the eggs she produces. Now when you look at this visually, this seems not to make sense. But here is how the conventional reasoning goes. You are going to want to reduce your taxes in your prime earning years, when you are in the highest tax bracket, and tax defer to your distribution years, when you will fall into a lower tax bracket.

When I parrot this line of reasoning, I follow by asking this question. Do you believe taxes will be higher tomorrow than they are today? The answer I get 100 percent of the time is that people do believe taxes will be higher tomorrow than they are today. I have been asking this question for years, over several presidencies and the answers are always the same. Even if we fast forward ten years and I ask the question again, people invariably believe that taxes will always be higher in the future than they are today. The government has an insatiable desire to grow; the populace has an insatiable desire for free stuff (even if it is not really free, the politicians marketing makes it appear to be free). When you combine those two things, we will have higher taxes. With this in mind, you may want to consider opportunities that reduce your taxes in the future, not just what reduces your taxes now.

The Roth IRA

The first big shelter in taxes is dependent on your understanding of after-tax versus pretax income. Keep in mind, inflation plus taxes takes a terrible toll on your gross income, taking out as much as one-third of your buying power with each pay cycle if you're working. So, when planning for the future, you want as much of your money free of taxes as possible. That allows its earnings to attack inflation without any tax handicap.

The easiest shelter available is the Roth IRA. It is after-tax money because you had to earn it as ordinary income first and pay tax on it before you could contribute it to the Roth. Why is this great tool? Because any money you deposit in a Roth is completely free of taxes later on when you withdraw it. That's right, no additional income tax to be paid. Both principal and earnings can collect at rates higher than inflation, and you owe nothing in taxes when you use that money in retirement. Add compounding interest (more on this later) and the possibilities are significant.

The beauty of using a Roth retirement account is that it avoids paying taxes altogether on both contributions and earnings. This is because those same taxes are already paid on the money you deposit. As a result, keeping within the limitations of the account use, and no new taxes will be owed. In essence, the Roth is technically a tax shelter for retirement savings, but it's not illegal like a bank account in some Caribbean bank offshore.

Roth accounts in general were first created in 1998 with the Roth Individual Retirement Account (IRA). The name was in honor of a Delaware senator who pushed the authorizing legislation through Congress. Today just about anyone can open a Roth account IRA and even greater benefits have become recently available:

- When converting a traditional retirement account to a Roth, MRD (Required Minimum Distributions) are excluded from the formula to determine allowable income limits (account holders are currently capped on how much adjusted gross income they can make and deposit to a Roth IRA).
- Inflation is not a factor in income limits. Roth IRA laws provide for inflation, indexing to those limits.
- Beginning in 2008, if you have a distribution from one of your traditional retirement accounts in your employer plan, you don't first have to put it in a traditional IRA. Instead it can go straight into a Roth IRA without penalty (translation—there is no tax bite for the transfer. This is a huge benefit).
- By 2010, there will no longer be an adjusted gross income limit before you can deposit via a Roth conversion, (you don't have to wait until you're making less money to be eligible).

The biggest shift in retirement account laws occurred in 2006 when Congress created the Roth accounts in 401(k) and 403(b) plans. This new option is very similar in function to the Roth IRA, but the big difference is that you can use it in conjunction with your employer retirement plan. That allows you to keep matching contributions from your employer. You don't have to wait until employment separation to get into a Roth account.

Overall, both types of Roth accounts make it easier to build, preserve, and use your retirement savings. We'll go over each in some detail below.

The Roth IRA is the single best gift that Congress ever gave to the American taxpayer. It allows us to build a retirement account tax-free, which can grow to incredible size. There is only one catch: you have to pay the income tax up-front. The Roth works opposite of a traditional IRA and other tax-deferred accounts (401(k) etc.). With the Roth IRA, you pay income tax when you put in the money and get no tax deduction. After that, all future growth and withdrawals are tax-free to you and your beneficiaries.

Why is it better to pay taxes now? The traditional IRA assumes you will be in a lower tax bracket when you withdraw your money. But this is a myth in today's world. Most people are in a higher tax bracket in retirement, given their retirement income, Social Security, and investment income combined. Thus, a Roth saves more money over the long run because the withdrawals when needed are tax-free and remain tax-free to beneficiaries. The only requirement to be effective is have the account a minimum of five years and be fifty-nine-and-a-half years old before taking withdrawals. Additionally, unlike a traditional account, you never have to take money out at age seventy-and-a-half. You can leave it in and let it grow. Only when the money is left to a nonspouse beneficiary, are the distributions then required.[38]

You are limited to $5,000 a year in contributions as of 2008 if your income is below $90,000 or $150,000 for married couples filing jointly ($6,000 if you are over the age of fifty). A minimum contribution should be made, even if it's only $25 a month, to get the five-year holding period going. Roth contributions are allowed regardless of age.[39]

To convert to a Roth, IRA from a traditional IRA, you need to pay the conversion tax first. If you do not pay it now, you or your beneficiaries will pay it later and likely at a higher rate. There is no limit, no gap, no ceiling on the amount that can be converted—if you're willing to pay the income tax. You can convert $10 million or $1,000. The limitation is that your annual income cannot be over $100,000 and you must be married filing joint. Married separate filers are out of luck for some reason. Individuals have the same $100,000 income cap. The income used is your Adjusted Gross Income (AGI).[40]

Home Ownership Benefits—The designers of the Roth IRA were cognizant of the home-ownership dream as well. Thus first-time home buyers can use their Roth for up to $10,000 for the purchase without tax penalty (including earnings). The only restrictions are time-wise in nature. You had to have owned the account for at least five years. The limitation is per person, so a married couple could double the benefit and withdraw up to $20,000, which more than qualifies for a down payment on a $300,000 home. Although this particular benefit generally does not apply to the target audience of this book, it will apply to your children. So encourage them to open one now.

Spousal Contributions: Roth IRA rules now also allow for spousal contributions, being cognizant of nonworking spouses needing to have a retirement cushion as well. The earning spouse can deposit for the other and still simultaneously deposit into their own Roth IRA without exceeding annual deposit limitations.

Early Withdrawals: There are penalties for taking your money out too soon, normally with retirement accounts, but with a Roth IRA, they don't apply on the contributions. So you can get to your money in a pinch. However, the IRS does take a bite out of earnings if they are withdrawn as well too early.

As we noted earlier, though, education expenses are exempted. So if an account holder had to withdraw earnings prior to age fifty-nine-and-a-half, he or she could do so tax-free as long as the money was used to pay college bills. It would definitely be smart to save receipts and billing invoices from schools to prove the case later to the IRS. Of course, none of this applies if the accountholder is already fifty-nine-and-a-half when the tuition needs to be paid.

Keep in mind, though, the more you take out before retirement, the less you have to compound on, which of course reduces your retirement nest egg later when you need it in your older years.

So let's see how using a Roth actually fends off taxes.

For example, let's say you start putting away a few dollars each year at the age of thirty-eight. You will retire at sixty-five. So you deposit basically $3,200 a year. It's under the $5,000 limit, but it's all the spare cash you can squirrel away. Now, take that annual deposit and compound it at a measly rate of 3.25 percent. It doesn't sound like much, right?

Your aggregate principal, the deposits, will total to $83,200. That's OK, but your *compounded* earnings and principal will total over, to get this . . . $133,000.

What?!?

Yep, and you would owe no taxes—I repeat, *no taxes*—on that amount!

Now imagine what happens if you're really serious about saving and you deposit to the annual Roth limit every year, and then do the same for spousal Roth account as well. You could easily be in the neighborhood of a tax-free $266,000 at the same measly 3.25 percent rate compounded. So if you can get better rates through smarter and more powerful investing, obviously the returns are much higher compounded over time.

By contrast, 401(k) and traditional IRA contributions are usually pretax money because you received a tax deduction on the portion of your salary you contributed (if you're under the annual AGI amount), and will pay tax later when the funds are withdrawn. Most money accumulating in tax-deferred retirement accounts is pretax funds.[41] Ugh, how's that for a bite! An inflation hit on your buying power and paying income tax on your retirement fund distribution. A double-whammy!

TAXES HIT EVERYONE

> "I'm proud to pay taxes in the United States, the only thing is, I could be just as proud for half the money"—Arthur Godfrey.

The typical American Family spends more each month on income taxes than on food, clothing, and transportation combined. Just earning $57,343 annually in income puts you in the top 25 percent of all taxpayers.

Take the example of John, age fifty-five.

His planned retirement income is:

IRA/401(k)	$30,000
Social Security	$13,000
Interest and Dividends from Investments	*$22,000*
So he has a Total Income of:	**$65,000**

However, income after taxes (25 percent tax bracket) for John is only $48,750. Now let's see what happens to his income when taxes go up:

Income after taxes (40 percent tax bracket) $39,000

Income is *reduced* by 20 percent from original $48,750

Reducing your tax risk means minimizing taxable income in retirement and maintaining maximum deductions. It needs to be an ongoing practice that you avoid paying unnecessary taxes when possible. That means:

- Using selective tax deferrals
- Minimizing Social Security taxes
- Minimizing estate taxes
- Generating tax-free income

Let's go back to John again and change a few variables. Let's switch his retirement approach to the Roth IRA.

Planned retirement income:

~~IRA/401(k)~~ Roth IRA	$30,000
Social Security	$13,000
~~Interest and Dividends from Investments~~	
Tax-free Income	*$22,000*
Total Income	**$65,000**

John's income after taxes (25 percent tax bracket) is $65,000. Now we adjust for taxes going up and he still has income after taxes (40 percent tax bracket) of $65,000. What happened? His retirement distribution income is coming from his Roth, so no taxes on it when he uses it. His social security is not penalized because his other monies are not earned income. As a result, he keeps the total.

So why in the world would anyone use a 401(k) or a traditional IRA?!? Well, there are some good reasons. Those include:

- You want to tax-shelter the money you earn especially if your employer is matching your contribution. Let's face it, a $1 for $1 match on a 401(k) is basically a 100 percent rate of return. Even a 50 percent match is a 50 percent rate of return. Even with taxes later on, you're still keeping 100 percent of your money so it's a good deal for income earners.
- You assume that your tax rate when you retire will be less than what it is now. This is a gamble that you will

be in a lower tax bracket in retirement. If your gamble wins, you get taxed less than right now. However, if you lose and many do since they earn more later on, you get taxed just as much or higher. Only you can decide how that will best work, and I have made it clear what my opinion on the matter is.

- You need an IRA account ready for when you rollover your 401(k) or similar from a former employer but you don't want to take distributions from it yet. By rolling over to a traditional IRA, you avoid taxes until such time that you actually do take withdrawals. Keep in mind that this only shelters the money until seventy-and-a-half years of age, at which time you will be required to take minimum distributions and pay taxes.

OK, so we now understand what taxes can do to a retirement. What about the here and now? What can one do to take the sting out of taxes so you can save for a retirement in the first place? Well, . . .

For starters, if you get a big refund each year, you're having too much withheld from your paycheck. In effect, you're giving the government an interest-free loan. Some people like to have a pile of cash come back to them all at once in a refund. Others believe any dollar they give away, even temporarily, is a sin. The question you need to ask yourself is:

If you did not withhold the money, would you save it up to collect the interest yourself? If not, and you would just spend it, then you really haven't gained anything in terms of savings. By letting the government to borrow it for a while, you now have a lump-sum amount that is much larger than any boost you gained in a monthly paycheck that was then spent right away. However, keep in mind that if you have too little withheld, you may be charged an underpayment penalty. You must pay 90 percent of what you owe for the tax year by the end of that year or an amount equal to

100 percent of your tax liability for the previous tax year, whichever is smaller. For most people, this is not a problem. Your employer is required to withhold for you, so the right amount is taken out already. However, if you are part of a two-income family, the company only withholds enough for your paycheck it does not know and cannot ask to figure out what they should be withholding for two incomes combined.

For those that make $100,000 or more in a year, then withholding becomes an issue. As you move into higher tax brackets, or you pick up side income, you can trip withholding penalties very quickly. The best way to avoid this is to make prepayments quarterly on your estimated tax level. If it ends up too much at year's end, you get it back in a refund since it applies as a credit against taxes owed for the year.

Also, keep in mind that not every dollar of your taxable income is taxed at the same rate. This tiered tax approach is because portions of your earned income fall into different tax brackets, which are assigned different tax rates. Generally speaking, the first dollar you make will be taxed at a lower rate than your last dollar. Your marginal tax rate is the tax bracket, at which the highest (or last) portion of your income is taxed.

Your combined tax bracket determines how much tax you'll owe on income from investments such as CDs and money market funds. Your combined bracket is the sum of your top (or marginal) federal tax rate and your top state income tax rate. It may be less if you itemize deductions since you will be able to deduct your state income tax on your federal return. This is technical mumbo-jumbo that basically says everything you earn in a year, including interest or gain from investments, is taxed as one lump amount of income for tax purposes. So if you earned $100,000, collected $5,000 in interest, and $5,000 in profits from mutual funds, you would be taxed at $110,000 total income.

Your adjusted gross income (AGI) is your total income minus certain "Above the line" deductions such as deductible IRA contributions, alimony payments, or health savings account contributions. Your AGI primarily determines whether or not you're eligible for tax breaks. Almost every break, be it a deduction, exemption, or a credit, has its own AGI limit. Your taxable income is your AGI minus exemptions and deductions. The less your taxable income, the less in taxes you'll owe. That's why it's in your best interest to take advantage of tax breaks where you can.

A credit is better than a deduction. A credit is a dollar-for-dollar reduction of the taxes you owe. A $100 credit means you pay $100 less in taxes. A deduction reduces the taxes you owe by a percent of every dollar you're allowed to deduct (remember our discussion about mortgages? Mortgage interest is a deduction which is less than the effect of paying it off, dollar for dollar). You calculate the worth of your deduction by multiplying your marginal (or top) tax rate by the amount of the deduction. If you're in the 25 percent tax bracket, a $100 deduction means you'll pay $25 less in taxes ($100 times 0.25).

Of course, you'll want to avoid common mistakes that will delay your refund, such as entering your social security number incorrectly, making a simple math error, or writing down the wrong address.

Your filing status is determined as of December 31 of the tax year. So even if you were only married for one day of 2005, you can no longer file as "Single." Married filers typically pay lower taxes if they file a joint return rather than separate returns. So unless you have a good reason to file separately from your spouse (one spouse owns his own business, for example), it's in your best interest to file together. The IRS also takes certain credits and deductions off the table if you file separately.

Student loans get treated similar to mortgages. The interest on them is deductible. You can deduct up to $2,500 in student-loan interest in 2005 if your modified AGI is less than $50,000 or $100,000 if you're married and file a joint return. The amount of the deduction begins to phase out once your income exceeds those levels and disappears entirely if you earn more than $65,000 or $130,000 and if you're married.

If you went to school last year, Uncle Sam will foot part of your tuition bill under the Hope or Lifetime Learning credit. You can use only one in any given year for each qualifying person. The Hope credit gives you up to 100 percent of your first $1,000 in tuition and fees and up to 50 percent of the second $1,000. It applies to the first two years of college and is worth up to $1,500. The Lifetime Learning credit gives you up to 20 percent of your tuition and fees up to $10,000. The credit maximum is $2,000.

If you made a job-related move, you might be able to write off your relocation expenses. To qualify, you must have moved at least fifty miles away. You can include the cost of getting yourself, your family and your possessions to your new home, including the cost for plane tickets, movers, rental trucks, and gas. If you were employed and looked for a new job within your field last year, you can write off the costs of your search, including travel to interviews, printing résumés, and employment agency fees. The catch: you can only write off job-search expenses if you itemize deductions on your tax return and if the expenses exceed 2 percent of your AGI.

The different ways to save on taxes are as varied as the tax code itself. You approach needs to attack the issue from multiple fronts. A successful financial plan hits taxes now and takes steps to avoid taxes in the future. Between smart tax filings today and using shelters such as a Roth IRA for the future, you can create a very powerful, effective tool to avoid unnecessary tax payment and hedge against inflation. And that's what you really want if your goals are to live comfortably in your retirement.

Avoid audits. They cost you money needlessly. You can reduce your chances of being audited by just filing—one of the best ways is to fill out your return completely, correctly, and on time every year. The most common and obvious audit finding is the tax filer who suddenly stops filing. It's like the one person who didn't show up to the office meeting; it's really obvious to the tax collectors.

One final remark in the area of taxes: if you're about ready to do anything, seek the advice of a professional. I had a client come into my office after selling a piece of property that he had purchased thirty years ago for under $100,000. He asked me how he could avoid the capital gains tax on the sale they made; the sale exceeded $1.2 million. So he was looking at capital gains taxes of 15 percent on the gain of $1.1 million. I looked them in the eye, and I said, "Before you sell the property . . . ," and then I began to outline several strategies which would have completely avoided the capital gains tax on that land, saving him $165,000. The problem was that he had already sold the property.

Although we have covered a lot of ground on this subject, we have in no way exhausted it. I will sum up this section by saying that all legitimate tax planning strategies fall into four basic categories.

1. Timing—reducing taxes by changing the year, in which income is received or deductions taken.
2. Shifting—reducing taxes by shifting income to someone in a lower tax bracket.
3. Investing—using investments to reduce taxes.
4. Use of tax law provisions—taking advantage of all tax law provisions.[42]

Finally, taxes are kind of like toothpaste being squeezed out of a tube. Once the toothpaste is outside, you can't put it back in. So make sure you know all your options before you do anything major that can have large tax implications, even if you're not sure. Seek the advice of a professional.

Rule #3: Diversify, Diversify, Diversify

You have heard the quip, "What are the three rules of real estate? Location, location, location." Our third rule is the same, Diversify, Diversify, Diversify. Or should I say, "Don't put all your nest egg in one basket."

A good definition of diversification is a wide selection of asset classes and sectors with dissimilar or noncorrelated price movements. However, the problem with this definition is that it does not include some of things that are necessary for a good, diversified portfolio. In order to potentially generate an appropriate level of growth, you need to pay close attention to your investment allocation. This is where diversification has a major impact. Or as Nobel Prize winner in Economics Merton Miller said, "Diversification is your buddy." I bet you were expecting something more erudite from a Nobel Prize winner.

To explain diversification and how difficult it can be, we're going to cover some bullets, specifically two sets of them. Real diversification requires:[43]

- Different Asset Classes—this includes things like large cap growth, large cap value, international, microcap, etc. They need to have disproportionate price movements or in other words, don't go down or up all at the same time.
- Multiple Sectors—this includes things like energy, consumer goods, entertainment, retail, real estate, commodities, military, etc.
- Nonduplication—owning lots of stuff doesn't mean you don't own the same stuff. For example, many portfolios may have multiple mutual funds. But then own the same stock amongst those multiple funds. For example, we did an analysis of a person with thirty mutual funds and found out that AT&T was owned in twenty-seven of them. This is not

diversification. If you own mutual funds, this is a problem you have and don't know it! (An overlap analysis will expose this.)

- Time Structure—the expectation of how long you're going to own each asset needs to be defined.
- Different Costs and Fees—a portfolio with a single management fee of 2 percent is not diversification. Many high quality products have different fee structures and combining them to generate the lowest possible overall fee should be the objective.
- Tax Strategies—different tax classifications require different distribution strategies. This needs to be figured into the overall plan.
- Noncorrelated Investments—it is important that part of the portfolio is not involved in the market at all. You want parts of your portfolio to make money regardless of market crashes that will occur, similar to what happened in 2008.
- Different "Inventory" from Different "stores"—if someone is telling you that you can accomplish all your goals with a single stock portfolio, a mutual fund portfolio, or a single product like a variable annuity, then, you need to find another financial advisor and quickly.
- Different Fees—commissions, management fees, spreads, are all ways of paying for products, nothing is free (CD's use spreads).

The major drawback is that all of this results in a lot of paperwork! Remember that I said that the standard (not inverted) triangle business model was the most difficult to implement?

How can we create a diversified portfolio? Typically, the traditional recommendation is to own a collection of equity mutual funds, or individually managed stock accounts.

This is way too simplistic of a portfolio and did not hold up well in 2008. This is what a vast majority of Americans own and why a vast majority of Americans distrust financial advisors and why I recommend a strategist and coach. I have a simple vetting tool. You hear about vetting all the time in politics. Vetting is a process of examination and evaluation, generally referring to performing a *background check* on someone before offering him or her, an employment. In addition, in *intelligence gathering*, *assets* are vetted to determine their usefulness.[44] When determining the usefulness of advice you are about to be given, keep in mind the Diversity Trinity, a great vetting tool.

The three parts of the diversity trinity are *in, within*, and *out*. I am going to use an example of Stocks to show how to use the Diversity Trinity to determine if your portfolio is properly diversified.

You decide to use publicly held companies as part of your portfolio so you will be *in* stocks. You would want to own multiple stocks, in multiple countries, in multiple asset classes, in multiple industries or sectors; you will be spread *within* those stocks. You then need to be in something not in stocks and have money *out* of stocks. Do not own any one stock, product, or strategy that exceeds 10 percent of your portfolio. For those that insist on owning gold (I promised I would show you how to own it) or CDs, then no more than 10 percent of what you own should be in those strategies. You still can use the Diversity Trinity if you chose to be *in* gold by owning gold producers, gold users, coins, bars, etc. (*within*).

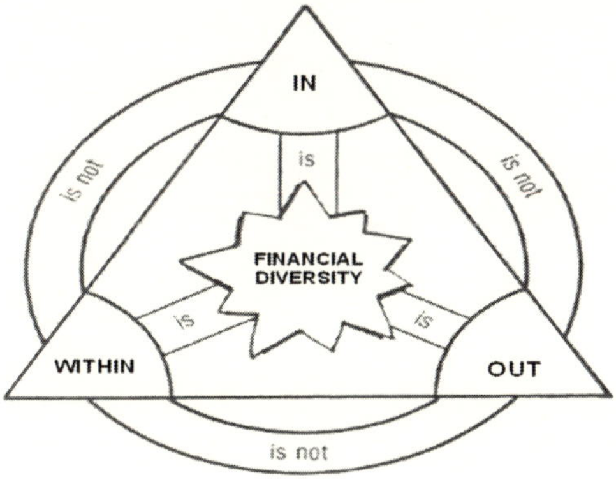

The only exception to the 10 percent rule is a *collection* of stocks because by their very nature they are diversified. It would be rationally impossible to argue that owning 12,000 to 14,000 stocks in twenty plus countries in every conceivable industry in 50 percent of your portfolio was not diversified. You should never own more that 10 percent of your portfolio in a *single* stock. If you disagree ask a former Enron or MCI employee.

Finally, if you are not convinced, King *Solomon*, the richest and wisest man to ever live, actually left us with some investment advice about proper diversification in Ecclesiastes 11:2. "Divide your portion to seven, or even to eight, for you do not know what misfortune may occur on the earth." I call this the ancient portfolio theory.

Dr. Harry Markowitz was a pioneer of modern portfolio theory. He wrote a doctorate paper in 1952, that won the Nobel Prize in Economics in 1990. The delay in acknowledgement was because it took nearly forty years for computer technology to advance to the point where his theories could be proven. Like Albert Einstein who wrote the black hole theory on the back of an envelope, it wasn't until forty years later that a Black Hole was actually discovered in space by the Hubble telescope. Mr. Markowitz, like Einstein, was truly ahead of his time.

Part of Markowitz's paper was the concept of the efficient frontier. It is a hypothetical graph that illustrates an optimal portfolio return for any given level of risk. A Markowitz efficient portfolio is one where no added diversification can lower the portfolio's risk for a given return expectation (alternately, no additional expected return can be gained without increasing the risk of the portfolio). The Markowitz efficient frontier is the set of all portfolios that will give the highest expected return for each given level of risk.

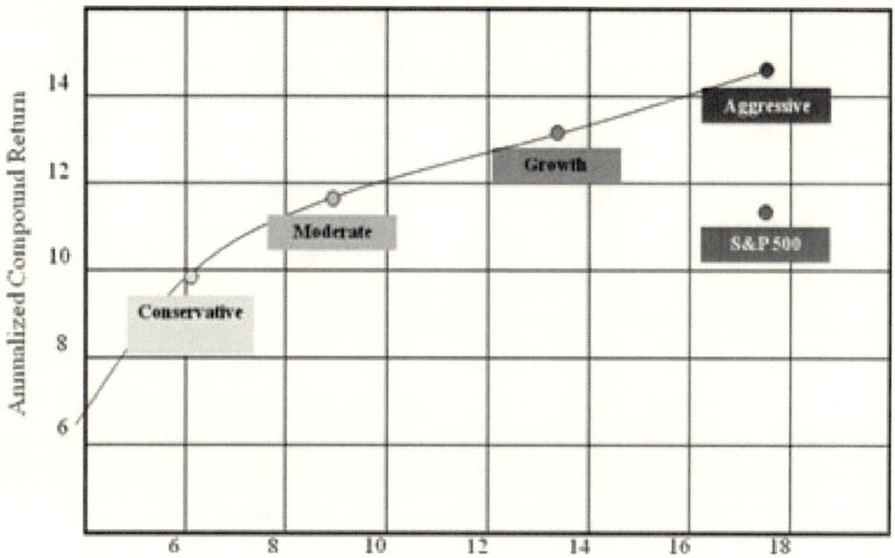

One Year Standard Deviation (Volatility)

Above is the Markowitz efficient frontier. It is a hypothetical graph that illustrates an optimal portfolio return for any given level of risk.

For example, we can take an investor who has 100 percent of their money in the S&P 500 and say, you have a historical rate of return of around 11 percent, and you have an historical volatility of over 17 percent. If you're comfortable with that level of return, why don't we move you straight across this graph to pick up essentially the same returns with one half of the volatility? Or, if you are comfortable with that volatility, we can just move you straight up the graph; pick up an extra 3 percent or 4 percent rate of return per year without any additional volatility in your portfolio.

A good advisor should be able to plot where your current investment portfolio falls on this efficient frontier. Without this measurement, not only do you not know where you are, but you have no way of knowing where you should be going.

In other words, if I don't know what you are cooking, how do you know if you have the right recipe? Have you ever been in a mall, where one of those big maps of the mall had a little red dot with an arrow that marked "You are here?" This is what this does for your portfolio. It says you are "Here."

In the early part of 2009, there were several articles that came out saying that modern portfolio theory is dead. The general thesis of these articles was that since the whole market melted down all at once, then, diversification doesn't work. Or stated differently, since the international and domestic stocks fell simultaneously, then MPT does not work. Both of these are what the intellectual world calls a strawman argument. A strawman argument is defined as a logical fallacy based on a misrepresentation of an opponent's position. MPT's main claim is that by adding asset categories with dissimilar price movement, it is possible to increase long-term expected return while reducing overall volatility. Nothing changed in 2008, and MPT held up very well when applied correctly. A lot of people and their advisors thought that if they had lots of mutual funds that all they had to do is treat it like Ronco's rotisserie oven. Set it and forget it! The primary problem is mutual funds are *not* diversified (go back to the beginning of this section if you missed it). Also, mutual funds are actively traded so you may be setting it and forgetting it, but the fund managers aren't.

Once again, modern portfolio theory is *not* dead . . . according to Harold Evensky, CFP, AIF, president of Evensky, and Katz Wealth Management in Coral Gables, Fla., the classic definition of MPT boils down to diversifying investments among different types of investments, each of which have unique characteristics, hence reducing the probability of sustaining a large loss. Unfortunately, the last eighteen months have challenged the theory. Disparate asset classes, with distinct risk profiles, all went down together. What went so terribly wrong? Evensky concludes: "It's not that MPT is invalid, it's that the application has been faulty."

According to Evensky: “The MPT model alone will not necessarily work in bear markets, or at least not using historical averages alone as inputs without other adjustments to forecast the return, volatility, and especially correlation.”[45]

Having Harold Evensky agree with me (or me with him) is like having Julia Child’s love for my cooking.

What You Can’t Not Know!

J. Budziszewski has a great book called, *What We Can’t Not Know*, it has to do with religious philosophy and has nothing to with finances. However, he argues, in the book, that we all have deep inside us a moral regulator—our conscience—that tells us right from wrong. This conscience is part of our human nature. I believe this is true of finances as well. It is the job of the financial industry to bombard you with messages to convince you to do what is counter-intuitive.

By doing this together, although they are not working together, they create a recipe for disaster. For example, in the food industry you will see a man with rippling muscles ending a hard work out with a soda or even a beer. This is counter intuitive to all that we know. Why put on the very calories that he has just worked so hard to take off? The goal of the beverage company is to tie athletic endeavors, which make you thirsty with their product that they claim is the best at quenching that thirst. Have you ever gulped down a sugary soda after a work out? After doing that you will realize, nothing quenches thirst like water and it is free! We know this to be true, but it is the role of the advertiser to change that belief and as a result our behavior.

If all the soda companies were all advertising that somehow there was a connection between being muscular and drinking soda, eventually this “Fact” would become a myth, if it was a widely held belief and it was wrong.

The financial industry has done an excellent job of spending its way into perpetuating several myths.

MYTH 1: STOCK PICKING

This is the belief that you can pick Microsoft before it becomes Microsoft. The idea that you can consistently pick any one stock or collection of stocks that will out earn the market is folly. It is no different than picking the right slot machine at the right time. This is where many people with gold fever fall. They feel like that one pick of gold that will be there, best bet. Note that word, bet. Stock picking is betting. It does not feel like betting because you can chart and graph past earnings, potential earnings, alphas, dividends, price to earnings ratios, and on, the list goes.

In cooking, all you have to do is follow a set of rules and you will know your outcome. You will always get a soufflé, casserole, or pie if you follow the recipe. There is another word for this. A word that sums up what can be tested and proven to have the same outcome each time it is tested. The word is science. When you marry gambling and science their child is a casino. When you marry stock picking with a bunch of charts and graphs you have the appearance of science, but it is still just gambling and you are betting against the house whose child IS science, not the appearance of science.

I was watching one of the premier horse races on a Saturday afternoon and there was a commercial for a Web site for horse race fans. It was an electronic racing forum. It tracked winnings (past earnings), potential (the parents of the horse), alphas (odds), dividends (stud fees), and price to earnings ratios (cost to winnings). It had cool fancy graphs and I was stunned just how similar it looked to several of the financial Web sites. I wonder if the company that produces the site is actually in the financial business and saw a natural fit. The bottom line is the future is unknowable; that is something you can bet on!

People with brain damage make better financial decisions. No, I am not kidding. Emotions really stab you in the back. A study by Loewenstein and colleagues did, in fact, find that people who were unable to feel emotions due to brain lesions were better investors than those with fully functioning brains.

Participants in the study were given $20 for a 20-round gambling game, then asked before each round if they wanted to bet $1 on a coin toss. If they won, they would earn $2.50. If they lost, they would lose their dollar. From a clearly logical perspective, the bet makes good financial sense.

In the end, people with brain damage invested in 84 percent of the rounds for average earnings of $25.70. However, those with "Normal" brains invested in only 58 percent of the rounds, for average earnings of $22.80.

Interestingly, the normal-brain participants' ability to experience fear actually held them back from making the best investment decisions.

"What we found out, through additional analysis, is that normal individuals were reacting emotionally to the outcome of the previous round," said Baba Shiv, an associate professor of marketing at the Stanford Graduate School of Business and coauthor of the study. "If they lost money, they got scared and had the tendency to fall back and decline to play further."

So either, become brain damaged, find someone who is brain damaged, or find a strategist and coach that will help you stop stock picking.

MYTH 2: MARKET TIMING

Most people will agree with me on the first one, but I get a lot more resistance on this one. The problem is that our emotions betray us. That is instead of buying low and selling high, we succumb to greed and fear. The tech bubble proved the greed factor in the 1990s as people got into the market late in the bubble and then violated the diversity rule by buying all tech stocks. *Dalbar* is an independent research firm that does massive studies on investor behavior tracks the *real* results that investors get. In 2007, they concluded a twenty-year study of tens of thousands of brokerage accounts for investors who have over $100,000 invested—so not just small, inexperienced folks.

Category	1988–2007 Annualized Return
S&P 500 Index	**11.81 percent**
Average Equity Fund Investor	4.48 percent
Systematic Equity Fund Investor	5.83 percent
Market Timer Equity Fund Investor	**(-1.35 percent)**
Inflation	3.04 percent

People think they can be rational investors, they can't. The numbers above tell the story. Emotions cloud rational thinking, this is something "You can't not know."

Here is even more proof. The chart below shows what would have happened if you missed just sixty of the best trading out of a possible 2,520 trading days. You go from 8 percent positive to 11 percent negative! That is just like getting out of the market for ninety days and waiting till it looks like it will recover. You can't recover after it has already recovered!

January 1, 1996 – December 31, 2006

2,520 Trading Days

	Return of S&P 500 Index	Growth of $10,000 Investment *
Fully Invested	8.33%	$22,252
Missed 10 best days	3.32%	$13,864
Missed 20 best days	-0.46%	$9,548
Missed 30 best days	-3.71%	$6,649
Missed 40 best days	-6.42%	$5,148
Missed 60 best days	-10.98%	$3,125

*Fact Set Research Systems
Based on initial investment of $10,000

I have heard there are employees that were given shares of Walmart stock and are now millionaires, does that mean if I buy Walmart stock I will become a millionaire? No they are *already* millionaires, I missed the opportunity. If you lock in losses and wait till the market recovers you will miss the opportunity as well. The best thing you can do for yourself is properly and prudently design your portfolio and to stay the course. If your portfolio is wisely designed, it will not go down as much as the ones that make the headlines and scare everyone. If your portfolio could have been on the news, you need to follow the advice I have given and/or find an advisor that does.

In the book *Rich Chick*, Michelle Matson makes an excellent point.

> Sometimes a Frog is just a Frog . . .
>
> Although investing is a long-term commitment, much like a relationship not all portfolios or investments are created equal. It can be very hard to know if you are getting what you need inside your portfolio.

> At times, investing can be compared to a frog and a prince. Of course, you always want to go for the prince. However, sometimes a frog is just a frog, and no matter how many times you kiss it, it's never going to turn into a prince. In the same way, if you end up with a portfolio or a frog that isn't made up of the right materials, no matter how long you stick with it, it may never yield the results you are looking for. That's why it's important for you to get a firm grip on all of the Rich Chick accessories so that you can use your newfound knowledge to find the right portfolio, like the perfect prince, you will gain years of satisfaction and growth that you never imagined possible. [46]

For you guys, sometimes a dog is a dog.

Myth 3: Track Record Investing

This is the idea that you can pick from the best mutual fund based on what is in the last years, last three years, last five years, last ten years, or even the inception to date numbers. Despite the prevalent, "Past performance is no indication of future results" disclaimer that is everywhere, we still seem to base our choices on past performance. Let me illustrate how ridiculous this is. Put yourself in a stadium with twenty thousand people and give each one, a coin to flip. After each flip all those with tails will sit down. After ten flips, there is a statistical probability that someone in the theatre is still standing. Does the person that flipped the coin heads ten times in a row have a special flipping ability? Should I bet that because he flipped ten times in a row that he will do it again? No! In fact, if he has flipped ten times in a row I would be even more worried that his lucky streak would end.

I met with someone that will not let go of a mutual fund that she has now owned for over twenty-five years and it has not done well for over fifteen years and has not made money for the last five years and to top it off each year she has to pay capital gains tax on a fund that has not made money in years. The market is random and unpredictable so if someone has done well in the past they are not likely to do well in the future just because in the past, they got lucky. This line of reasoning will get you in less trouble than buying on good past performance.

The irony is that going down the path that the myths lead is far more stressful than the approach I have outlined. What I have outlined is like the weather, not a slot machine. I don't know what the weather is going to be like next May in Dallas, TX, but I can look at the history and know that May is the rainiest month of the year. Science measures the weather patterns and then records what they consistently have done in the past. Based on this history I can determine what the weather is likely to do in the future. I know with near certainty that in August it is hot in Dallas it will be hot,

A few years back the gulf coast had the most active hurricane season it has ever seen. Many weather alarmists claimed it was going to be like this every year. If the alarmists were financial companies, they would have exploited the one good year or the one bad year in this case to encourage you to bet that the next year would be exactly the same, but that just isn't how the market works, or the weather. There are market anomalies just like there are weather anomalies. It is better to use science and math to build your portfolios then base it on past anomalies.

TIME HORIZON

A time horizon, also known as a planning horizon, is a fixed point of time in the future at which point certain processes will be evaluated or assumed to end. It is necessary in accounting, finance, or risk management to assign a fixed time horizon so that alternatives can be evaluated for performance over the same period of time. Examples of time horizons would include:[47]

- A new car (investment period: two years, drawdown: none)

- A house down payment (investment period: three to five years, drawdown: none)
- College costs (investment period: six to ten years, drawdown: several years)
- Retirement with investing late in career (investment period eleven to fifteen years, drawdown: to age ninety-five or longer)
- Retirement with investing early in career (investment period sixteen years or more, drawdown: to age ninety-five or longer)

Now throw in the concept of compounding. Compound interest is the concept of adding accumulated interest back to the principal, so that interest is earned on interest from that moment on. The act of declaring interest to be principal is called compounding (i.e., interest is compounded). A loan, for example, may have its interest compounded every month: in this case, a loan with $100 principal and 1 percent interest per month would have a balance of $101 at the end of the first month. This is why, all debt is so bad. It is compounding, working against you.

Albert Einstein, arguably one of the most intelligent people who ever lived, was asked what he thought was the greatest of mankind's discoveries. His answer: compound interest. He went so far as to call it the eighth wonder of the world. So do you want this wonder working for you or against you?

Here is a fun example of the power of compounding interest. If the Native American tribes that accepted goods worth sixty guilders for the sale of Manhattan in 1626 had invested the money in a Dutch bank at 6.5 percent interest, compounded annually, then in 2005 their investment would be worth over €700 billion (around USD $1 trillion), more than the assessed value of the real estate in all five boroughs of New York City. With a 6.0 percent simple interest however, the value of their investment today would have been €100 billion (1/7th as much!).

Compound interest was once regarded as the worst kind of usury, and was severely condemned by Roman law, as well as the common laws of many other countries.

Richard Witt's book, *Arithmetical Questions*, published in 1613, was a landmark in the history of compound interest. It was wholly devoted to the subject (previously called *Anatocism*); whereas previous writers had usually treated compound interest briefly in just one chapter in a mathematical textbook. Witt's book gave tables based on 10 percent (the then maximum rate of interest allowable on loans) and on other rates for different purposes, such as the valuation of property leases. Witt was a London mathematical practitioner and his book is notable for its clarity of expression, depth of insight and accuracy of calculation, with 124 worked examples.[48] [49]

Under Islamic religion, the Qur'an explicitly mentions compound interest as a great sin, even though Muslims all over the world continue using it. Interest known in Arabic as "Riba" is considered wrong:

> Oh, you who believe, you shall not take Riba, compounded over and over. Observe God, that you may succeed (Qur'an 3:130).

Once again do you want it working for you or against you?

Back to our examples for those who use compounding, using an average 8 percent interest rate for the rest of your life, the value of your $300,000 IRA will double every nine years (72/8=9), so that by the time you reach eighty-six, your $300,000 IRA will have doubled four times and be worth $4.8 million. The first time it doubles, it will go to $600,000, then, after another nine years to $1.2 million, then to $2.4 million, then to $4.8 million. If you start with a $500,000 IRA at the age of fifty and use the same 8 percent interest rate, your IRA will grow $8 million by the time you reach eighty-sixty. And a $1 million IRA would grow to a staggering $16 million.

Of course, I am using big numbers to make the point about how powerful compounding is, but let's look at it in an unique way. If you have $100,000 and you were to be living off the interest of this account of 5 percent a year for the next ten years you would make $5000 a year. In ten years you would have taken $50,000 in income. This is how most so called financial planners and advisors build portfolios. They put all your money in a pile and expect the interest, dividends, and growth to pay the bills. Now what if you did not take the money and just left it in the account, would you have $150,000? No, you would have $162,889! You added over $12,000 to your account by compounding that is an increase of over 20 percent just by holding it and not spending. That extra $12,000 cost you nothing, it was a gift from compounding. So why don't more advisors work compounding into their plan for you? Let's ask the question another way, if your planner was paid a commission to build your plan around compounding, would your plan have it as an integral part?

Year	Value	Growth	Total
1	$100,000	$5,000	$105,000
2	$105,000	$5,250	$110,250
3	$110,250	$5,513	$115,763
4	$115,763	$5,788	$121,551
5	$121,551	$6,078	$127,628
6	$127,628	$6,381	$134,010
7	$134,010	$6,700	$140,710
8	$140,710	$7,036	$147,746
9	$147,746	$7,387	$155,133
10	$155,133	$7,757	$162,889

But what if you need the $5000 and can't just leave it to compound? Glad you asked! Take $50,000 and put it in an account earning 5 percent. Every year you earn 5 percent and you will be taking 5,000 out. It will take fourteen years and nine months before the money is gone and by then the other $50,000 has compounded at 5 percent to 103,440. It seems like a lot of work for an extra $3440 over ten years (another reason commission driven reps don't do this). First of all, it is not a lot of work if it is your money. What would you prefer the extra $3440 or not? Second, with a time horizon of fourteen plus years you could take more risk and potentially get better returns. If you follow the advice laid out so far, you could increase your risk slightly and get a return of 7 percent. Only 2 percent extra in returns would turn your $50,000 into $137,021! Get 9 percent returns and now you have $180,561! This is the power of . . .

SEGMENTING

You've probably heard of the concept of "laddering" in the context of CDs. This basically means, you systematically buy CDs with your investments in such a way that when they mature you have a regular flow of cash while still keeping most of your money invested. Here's how laddering CDs works:

You go to the bank with $25,000 and buy a $5,000 one-year CD, a $5,000 two-year CD and so on until your last $5,000 buys you a five-year CD. Each year is a rung on the ladder. When the one-year CD matures, you reinvest that money in a five-year CD because by that time your five-year CD has four years left until it matures. As each year's CD comes due, you roll it into a five-year CD. The laddered CD program helps give you more liquidity while offering a more stable source of income.

Bonds can be structured the same way. A bond ladder is a strategy that attempts to minimize risks associated with fixed-income securities while managing cash flows for the individual investor. Specifically, a bond ladder, which attempts to match cash flows with the demand for cash, is a multi-maturity investment strategy that diversifies bond holdings within a portfolio. It reduces the reinvestment risk associated with rolling over maturing bonds into similar fixed-income products all at once. It also helps manage the flow of money, ensuring a steady stream of cash flows throughout the year.

Suppose you had $50,000 to invest in bonds. By using the bond ladder approach, you could buy five different bonds each with a face value of $10,000 or even ten different bonds each a with face value of $5,000. Each bond, however, would have a different maturity. One bond might mature in one year, another in three years, and the remaining bonds might mature in five-plus years-each bond would represent a different rung on the ladder.

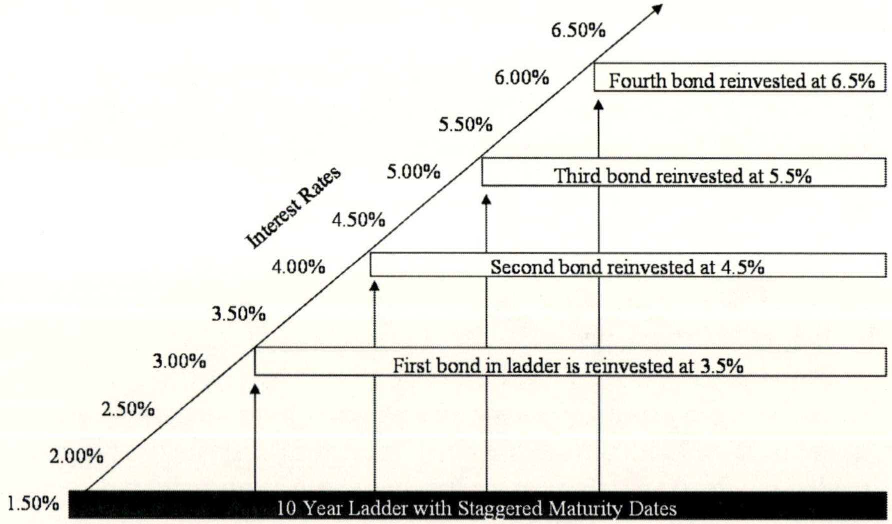

There are two main reasons to use the ladder approach. First, by staggering the maturity dates, you won't be locked into one particular bond for a long duration. A big problem with locking yourself into a bond for a long period of time is that you can't protect yourself from bull and bear bond markets. If you invested the full $50,000 into one single bond with a yield of 5 percent for a term of ten years, you wouldn't be able to capitalize on increasing or decreasing interest rates.

For example, if interest rates hit a bottom five years (at maturity) after purchasing the bond, then your $50,000 would be stuck with a low interest rate if you wanted to buy another bond. By using a bond ladder, you smooth out the fluctuations in the market because you have a bond maturing every year, (or thereabouts).

The second reason for using a bond ladder is that it provides investors with the ability to adjust cash flows according to their financial situation. For instance, going back to the $50,000 investment, you can guarantee a monthly income based upon the interest payments from the laddered bonds by picking ones with different maturity dates. This is more important for retired individuals because they depend on the cash flows from investments as a source of income. If you are not dependent on the income, by having steadily maturing bonds, you will have access to relatively liquid money. If you suddenly lose your job or unexpected expenses arise, then you will have a steady source of funds to use as required.

When you plan out your investments, you want them to be organized and invested in the same manner as laddered bonds or CDs. That means all along the time horizon, you have regular intervals where your money earns a profit, is available for liquidity, and can be systematically invested again.

So how do you actually make it happen? Let's go back to bonds as an example. The ladder itself is very simple to create, and just picture an actual ladder:

> **Rungs**: By taking the total dollar amount that you are planning to invest and dividing it equally by the total number of years for which you wish to have a ladder, you will arrive at the number of bonds for this portfolio, or the number of rungs on your ladder. The greater the number of rungs, the more diversified your portfolio will be and the better protected you

will be from any one company defaulting on bond payments.

Height of the ladder: The distance between the rungs is determined by the duration between the maturities of the respective bonds. This can range anywhere from every few months to a few years. Obviously, the longer you make your ladder, the higher the average returns should be in your portfolio since bond yields generally increase with time. However, this higher return is offset by reinvestment risk and the lack of access to the funds. Making the distance between the rungs very small reduces the average return on the ladder, but you have better access to the money.

Materials: Just like real ladders, bond ladders can be made of different materials. One straightforward approach to reducing exposure to risk is investing in different companies, but investments in products other than bonds are sometimes more advantageous depending on your needs. Debentures, government bonds, municipal bonds, Treasuries, and certificates of deposit—each having different strengths and weaknesses—are all different products that you can use to make the ladder. One important thing to remember is that the products in your ladder should not be redeemable (or callable) by the issuer. This would be the equivalent to owning a ladder with collapsible rungs.

The key to the ladder's success for your investments is commitment. You need to make sure the ladder matches your long-term road map and you need to stick with it. If you're going to have an aberration, then you need to repair the cycle when you can so that the results produce consistently down the road. This design should insure a steady income stream when your investments mature, giving you the luxury of choice to either reinvest or use the income as needed.

You may think at this point I am a big fan of bonds. I'm not. Bonds are frequently laddered so I have used them as a reference point to explain laddering not to recommend bonds.

Now that you understand the concept of laddering, let's move on to the concept of segmenting, which is simply a variation of laddering. What we do with segmenting, is we create four basic segments of your portfolio, similar to the rungs on the ladder. Each segment is five years, planning a total of twenty years. The final segment is designed to replace the entire strategy. So as we grow and spend the first three segments, the fourth segment is growing aggressively and is intended to replace the initial investment adjusted for inflation and grown the overall portfolio. This will grow beyond the traditional methods of building a big pile and take what you need to live because it allows the time horizon on a large block of the portfolio to be stretched, which allows for more risk. Add the higher returns that typically come with higher risk (over time) to the impact of compounding interest and you have a recipe for success.

Warren Buffett said "What's needed is a sound intellectual framework for decisions and the ability to keep emotions from corroding that framework." Segmenting helps us do that. In 2008 when the markets were plummeting, my clients did not worry. This does not mean, they were not bothered by the fact that their stock portfolios were going down. They just realized that the stocks were part of a plan an "Intellectual framework," which allowed them to maintain the discipline and avoid the emotional reactions that watching the news everyday would create. I did get a couple of calls and I was able to coach my clients with one suggestion, Stop watching the news! I recommended the book, *How the News Makes Us Dumb: The Death of Wisdom in an Information Society* by C. John Sommerville. I would then remind them that the stock portfolio was *designed* not to be used for sixteen years. sixteen years is a real long time. Think about what has happened in sixteen years, the Internet had not created any wealth, Google, Ebay, and Amazon did not exist. It is silly to worry about the meltdown no matter how dramatic it was. Those reading this book probably already have forgotten the hysteria that was going on in October of 2008. Newspaperman Malcolm Muggeridge once said, "News is old things happening to new people."[50]

The typical refrain I would get from the public, that did not have a coach was, "This time is different!" Well, let me put that emotional response to rest with some headlines from Business Week in the 1970s, "The U.S. banking system has been stretched very nearly to the limit." "Now even nations are in danger of default." "The worldwide threat of financial instability rises." "The slide is steep, with *no* end in sight." All these quotes were from 1974-1975. My favorite quote from 1970, "For automakers, 1970 was the toughest year in at least a decade. Buyers spurned big models in favor of less profitable compacts, minicars, and fast-increasing imports."—*Time Magazine.*[51] Malcolm Muggeridge was right.

I digress, so back to segmenting.

After we have established how much money we need to live on monthly and adjusted that numbers for inflation, we then build the Segments.

- The First Segment of the plan consists mostly of liquid and low risk investments. The reason for this is that the assets have to be available for the next five years. This is the money that my first five years of retirement is going to come from. I can't afford a market downturn to erode these assets so they must be in something that is relatively safe and readily available because my monthly expenses will be paid from this first segment. Although I can easily make minor adjustments to my monthly needs, a market downturn like we experienced in 2008 would be impossible to adjust to in the first segment.

- The Second segment is the second five years of my retirement, years six through ten. I can take a little bit more risk here, because I have at least five years before, I will need this money. But at the same time, the average market cycle is five years. So I have to be careful because there is not a lot of time to make adjustments and the money needs to be available when I need it.
- The Third Segment is years eleven through fifteen. I can begin to take more risk in this segment. I will not need the money for ten years and will typically have seen two market cycles by the time I get to this money and the cash is needed.
- The Fourth and final segment, which is years sixteen through twenty, is typically where we build a market-based portfolio. Once again, diversification is the key. We don't just use stock portfolios exclusively in this last segment, but it is the bulk of what we will do in this segment. Depending on the asset level, there are some pretty sophisticated noncorrelated investments with low to medium standard deviations (remember standard deviation is a measurement of risk), that we can use here as well as some roll-the-dice type strategies. If you want to gamble with gold this is where you can do it. This intellectual will help keep your emotions at bay and get you closer to the elusive peace of mind.

Protect Yourself

Why do you think financial scams work so well even today with all the twenty-four hour news exposing major fraud? There are two basic reasons; the first is because people are lazy. They don't want to work at investing their money, and research takes work. Don't fool yourself, you need to read reports, results, monitor performance, and learn concepts regularly so that you can know, at the very least, that a fund that returns 12 percent every year with no risk can't be real (this was Madoff's claim). Stanford International touted "Improbable, if not impossible" returns for its CDs, the SEC said in a civil complaint.[52] Reading this book and implementing the strategies I have outlined is simple, but not easy. It takes time and effort. Aside from needing a lazy "Mark," as they say, they will always appeal to the emotions of fear or greed. That is another reason that the framework we recommend, has to be intellectual.

Most of us like to believe that we use logic when making important decisions in life. We are taught to value reason, common sense, and sound judgment. Unfortunately, being human means emotions will inevitably seep into our decisions. This is not necessarily a bad thing, but we need to diligently guard against our emotions distorting the factual data. When emotions drive our decision making, we tend to overweight the data that supports our emotions (or gut feelings) while simultaneously underweighting data that contradicts those feelings.

Evidence of this is seen in the news that prominent financier Bernard Madoff has been arrested for running what he allegedly called "A giant Ponzi scheme." The Securities and Exchange Commission (SEC) charged in a civil complaint losses to investors may run as high as $50 billion.

It's potentially the largest such schemes ever uncovered—nearly five times larger than the fraud that drove WorldCom into bankruptcy in 2002.

Madoff, a former chairman of the NASDAQ Stock Market, allegedly deceived wealthy investors who thought they were reliably earning 2 percent or more per month on their money even when financial markets were performing poorly.

Madoff, for decades headed Bernard L. Madoff Investment Securities LLC, a Wall Street firm that "Makes a market" in securities, meaning that it puts buyers and sellers of privately-traded equities together. That firm's operations were separate from the money management services Madoff provided for high-net-worth individuals, many of whom have been wiped out.

So how does something like this happen and how do you prevent it from happening to you? While the press points the finger everywhere, where it belongs, I can sum up the problem in one word.

Custody.

Madoff had custody of the accounts so he controlled the numbers his investors saw. He also controlled the numbers the auditors saw so when they didn't see anything wrong they did not do anything. How could they have known the numbers were completely fabricated? If you were to use a custodian that was different than the person managing your money this problem is immediately eliminated (assuming no collusion between parties—yes even that can happen). In other words, if I am buying and selling stocks for you inside of *my* account it is easy to commit fraud. But, if I am buying and selling stocks inside *your* account, held somewhere like Schwab Institutional, who reports on all my activity whether or not I want them to, you are protected in a way none of Madoff's investors were.

Most people are now thinking that it can't be that simple so allow me to complicate it. Here is a variation of what was sent by many custodians to their clients (the financial advisors) to explain how they protect the consumer, and the advisor:

How a Good Advisor distinguishes their operation from Madoff & Company:

1. They work with an independent registered investment advisor (RIA) regulated by the Securities Exchange

Commission (SEC), unlike Madoff's company which operated as an unregulated hedge fund for most of the time. There was no similar regulatory oversight, at least not until 2004 when he agreed to register as an RIA. They also make sure they are not affiliated with your custodian or with the brokerage firm that holds your investments and handles your trades, which was apparently not true of the Madoff business model.

2. An RIA submits to periodic inspections by the SEC at the federal or the state level. After becoming an RIA, Madoff apparently never did undergo a full SEC audit.
3. An independent advisor does not have the ability to hold the client's assets, nor do they have full power of attorney, as per the client's authorization. They only have the ability to affect trades in client accounts, charge advisory fees, and request checks payable to the client sent to the client's address of record. Madoff apparently had the ability to convert assets or transfer ownership of assets from one account to another and from one firm to another, so he had unimpeded control. An RIA should require the authority of the owner of the assets to accomplish these things.
4. Custodians are SEC registered, regulated by the Financial Industry Regulation Authority (FINRA) and the Municipal Securities Regulation Board (MSRB), different regulators than those which oversee the advisors business, which affords additional layers of regulatory oversight and protection for the client.
5. FINRA reviews custodial businesses independently of any review of an advisors business by the SEC. Most custodians report daily and monthly on a number of trading and asset metrics and the custodians undergo periodic inspections.
6. By regulation, custodians calculate net capital monthly, or daily if there's any question, and they must notify FINRA and the SEC if it comes within 120 percent of our minimum required capital. (Hedge funds have no similar requirement. They can lose all their clients' money.)

Custodians file a full statement of financial condition quarterly with the SEC and FINRA.

7. Items 4, 5, and 6, above also apply to clearing firms which many custodians have, which is also an independent broker/dealer. The clearing firm's (Pershing is the largest) Statement of Financial Condition is sent to clients at least annually, and it is available online.
8. Some large investment banking firms with problems have very complicated portfolios. Their balance sheets can look fine one day but, as we have seen, they can be bankrupt the next. In the case of some of the big wirehouse firms, it seems that no one really knew what all the risks were. They ran complicated businesses, acting as both custodians and investment bankers. By contrast, the relative "Simplicity" of a custodial business limits risk.

Like I said earlier, it is all about one word: *custody.*

Also, the Diversity Trinity would have minimized the Madoff effect. The rule of no more than 10 percent in any one strategy would have kept many in much better shape.

Part III
Delusions we Buy, and the Ones We Already Own

Amusing Ourselves TO Death

Amusing Ourselves to Death: Public Discourse in the Age of Show Business (1985)—Neil Postman.

Postman distinguishes the *Orwellian* vision of the future, in which *totalitarian* governments seize individual rights, from the vision offered by *Aldous Huxley* in *Brave New World,* where people medicate themselves into bliss and voluntarily sacrifice their rights. Postman sees television's entertainment value as a "*Soma*" for the contemporary world, and he sees contemporary mankind surrendering its rights in exchange for entertainment.

The essential premise of the book, which Postman extends to the rest of his argument(s), is that "Form excludes the content," that is, a particular medium can only sustain a particular level of ideas. *Rational argument,* an integral component of print typography, cannot be conveyed through the medium of television because "Its form excludes the content." Because of this shortcoming, politics and religion get diluted, and "News of the day" is turned into a commodity. The presentation most often de-emphasizes quality; all data becomes burdened to the far-reaching need for entertainment. Since television is programmed for maximum ratings, its content is determined by commercial feasibility, not critical acumen. Television in its present state, Postman says, cannot sustain any of the conditions needed for honest intellectual involvement and rational argument.[53]

Postman spends most of his time targeting the news media, but I am confident after reading his book, had he lived long enough to see what the financial media has become, that he would agree with Ms. Quinn's assessment of the financial media.

In 1995, Jane Bryant Quinn made this comment about the financial media in Newsweek, "As consenting adults in the privacy of their homes, Americans are indulging themselves in investment porn. Shameless stories about performance tickle our prurient financial interest." Quinn and Postman get what the media is about. It is designed to "Sell" newspapers, books, magazines advertising time, and products—*not* to help you make good investing decisions. Bottom line is that they are in the ratings business not the investment business.

In our quest for peace of mind we lazily flip a switch and turn to various sources of so-called expert information. These messages tend to be based on hype and rhetoric designed to manipulate our emotions. Instead of offering knowledge and clarity (which would be boring), they often provide conflicting advice, useless propaganda, and confusing hyperbole. The financial media is often specifically geared to activate and intensify the instinctual urges (fear and greed) which drive emotional decisions by the investor. In other words, like Ms. Bryant said, "Investment pornography." Most rational people would not consider getting long-term relationship advice from a magazine filled with pictures of people in various states of undress. So why get portfolio advice in the same manner?

Emotions and investor pornography are not the only way we delude ourselves into believing we do not need help from a financial strategist and coach. There is the ever present pride and over confidence. If you were to ask a room full of people if anyone of them is a bad driver, no hands will go up. It is strange that no one thinks that they are a bad driver, but everyone knows that there are bad drivers. I call this the bad driver paradox.

The "Do it yourself" investor is the toughest of all the people I meet with, because it is easier to convince someone that the "Other advisor" should be doing better than it is to convince the DIY'er that they should be doing better. They are frequently over confident in their own ability. They fall victim to the myths we have already discussed. Dalbar, Inc., is a leading financial services research firm that has conducted multiple studies with regard to investor behavior. We referenced to the most significant study earlier when we discussed market timing. Dalbar's most significant finding is that regardless of how well any particular investment may perform, the average investor is unlikely to realize the same return. This is the investor paradox. There is overwhelming evidence that individual investors can't beat the market yet they still believe they can. The delusion that creates the investor paradox is far more damaging than the bad driver paradox.

One of the things that happen to the individual investor that contributes to the investor paradox is, "Knowing" an outcome of some event or stock pick. It is the same thing that happens with the Monday morning quarterback phenomenon. This makes it easy to delude ourselves with confidence that we could have predicted the outcome with certainty. In postgame sports talk shows, the hosts and callers have convinced themselves that they knew, in advance, that a particular game strategy would fail, they even take the time to give evidence, like they saw a similar play in a similar instance in some game and it had the same outcome. Endless hours are spent on the air second-guessing the coaches and teams because, in hindsight, these "Monday Morning Quarterbacks" have such a clear perspective of what the winning strategy should have been. Ironically they only know what did not work, not what would have actually worked. Does anyone really believe these people had a clear idea of what the strategy should have been prior to the game? Of course not. Otherwise one of these "Experts" would have been hired as the coach or would have made a fortune betting on the game.

You can see hindsight bias at play whenever you hear someone say, "I knew that was going to happen." It is a commonplace tendency, and we've all done it. However, the fact of the matter is that none of us can predict actual outcomes in the future with any level of certainty or consistency. Only in hindsight does it become crystal clear. After all as the saying goes, hindsight vision is 20/20.

Hindsight bias focuses on past events and lulls us into believing that we had it all figured out. The phenomenon of hindsight bias is dangerous in investing because it sets up unrealistic expectations for the future.

Hindsight Bias Facts[54]

Between 1977-1989, Fidelity Magellan got higher returns than the S&P 500 for eleven of thirteen years. If we compare these statistics to the random flip of a coin, we find there is only 1 percent chance of observing eleven or more heads in thirteen flips of a coin. Using this analogy, it seems as if Peter Lynch, who managed the Magellan fund during this period, was clearly demonstrating skill vs. random luck.

Such thinking is one of the pitfalls of hindsight bias, however it is easy enough to look back from 1989 and see that Magellan was the big winner, but did we know at the beginning of the period (in 1977) that Lynch was going to have this long winning streak?

To determine whether Lynch truly demonstrated skill vs. luck during this time period, we can find the answer to a simple math question.

> **Question**: What are the chances that some mutual fund manager, among the total of five hundred managers, would beat the S&P 500 in eleven of thirteen years?

> **Answer**: 99.7 percent. Had we asked the same question at the outset, we would have known that over eleven or more of the upcoming years, some mutual fund manager would consistently beat the S&P 500. It is only the effect of hindsight basis that leads us to believe that we could have known that Peter Lynch would turn out to be the lucky winning manager.

Shooting streaks[55]

Athletes go on hot streaks (and cold streaks) at times in their careers. For example, a basketball player can experience a shooting streak where every shot seems to whoosh through the hoop; nothing seems to go wrong. Or so it would appear, especially as the announcers excitedly comment on and validate the spectacle.

And yet, statistics indicate otherwise. While we watch and see "Hot streaks," hard numbers show that players are just as likely to make the shot after scoring as they are to make the shot after missing. In fact, if we believe the numbers, there are no "Streaks" at all, simply random spurts with no consistent pattern.

As human beings, we are inclined to classify events, happenings, or activities that we don't readily understand. Therefore, we intuit patterns that hold no substantiation. We mistakenly perceive relationships where none exist. This is called false patterning.

Just as sports fanatics can get caught up in an athlete's apparent "Hot streak," investors are easily convinced that the market (or a certain investment in the market) is going to follow a particular pattern. This tendency is potentially harmful in investing because it leads to a mistaken sense of certainty about what is going to occur in the future.

False Patterning Facts

The simple fact that investment magazines continually publish and report on mutual funds' performance is based on the illusion that past performance is related to future performance. As documented by the esteemed economist Burton Malkiel, professor at Princeton University and author of *A Random Walk Down Wall Street*, "Randomness is a difficult notion for people to accept. When events come in clusters and streaks, people look for explanations and patterns" and as can be read in the fine print of most mutual fund prospectuses or investment literature: "Past performance does not indicate and is not a guarantee of future performance."

More Evidence of Overconfidence

> " . . . the beliefs, biases and preferences that influence individuals . . . are optimism, overconfidence, hindsight, confusing chance with skill and ignoring the big picture . . . A former student of mine, Terrence Ogden, looked at the prices of stocks one year after individual investors bought and sold them through retail brokerage firms. Less the transactions costs, the stocks that were sold did better on average by 3.4 percent, which means that people are making decisions, on average, quite badly. They are throwing away, on average, close to 5 percent of their investments-3/4 percent plus transactions costs. This is solid evidence that people are optimistic and overconfident."

—Daniel Kahneman, psychologist, Dow Jones Asset Management, November/December 1998

Necessary Lies[56]

Necessary lies are the seemingly harmless little things we tell ourselves when we're doing something we know we shouldn't do. Inherently, we can sense when we are involved in behavior that could be considered reckless or irresponsible. After years of conditioning, there is often an internal voice whispering that we are breaking the rules. Natural responses to this kind of self-condemnation are rationalization and justification. Even if we are only talking to ourselves, we are hardwired to excuse and defend our own behavior. This tendency only becomes more pronounced in situations in which we feel someone else might be judging our behavior. These are the times when we generously apply necessary lies. These seemingly minor falsehoods let us off the hook for doing what we know we shouldn't.

Brutal Honesty

The remedy to necessary lies is brutal honesty. If you are ever going to be a realistic investor, then you must be willing to admit your own falsehoods. Think about your own investing situation. How have you been fooling yourself?

In what ways have you been investing imprudently or irrationally while convincing yourself that "This time is really different?" Do you need a coach that will be brutally honest with you? Someone that will show you that you are not being honest with yourself?

> "We should be careful to get out of an experience only the wisdom that is in it—and stop there; lest we be like the cat that sits down on a hot stove lid. She will never sit on a hot stove lid again—and that is well; but also she will never sit down on a cold one anymore."—Mark Twain.

Unfortunately, the DIY investor with all the proclivities mentioned above is not as prevalent as the pessimist. I am starting to believe that the number one disease of the American populace is pessimism. That or we are addicted to bad news. Either way, the outcome is a paralysis. These people naturally tend to remember negative experiences (i.e., losing money) more than they do positive ones (making money). As a result, after a couple of losing streaks a person may become afraid of investing altogether, and miss out on good opportunities. Or even worse they see that something bad has happened to someone else and decide they want no part of anything related to it.

Imagine you had a really bad pasta dish at a restaurant. Would you stop eating *all* pasta, anywhere at any time? No! You can rationally assess that this was a singular bad experience with pasta and is unlikely to be repeated. You might even try to figure out why it was a bad experience, was it the sauce, the restaurant or some other factor. Unfortunately the emotions of investing are not nearly as rational. Losing money has a far more emotional response than a bad pasta dish and it is akin to not only not eating any pasta at any restaurant, but no longer eating at restaurants.

The two feelings that trip up investors the most are fear and greed. We often can do great when we are paper-trading, but when actual money is on the line we may hold back from making the right decision based on fear, while holding on to an investment too long based on greed.

The end result, when you make emotional investment decisions is you may be putting your finances on the line. As humans we absolutely have to have something outside ourselves that keep us on the path that goes where we want to go. This is true morally, this is true physically and this is true for our money.

Basically, we need a financial coach. Jeff Spadora, a director at an organization called Halftime, has distilled a definition of coaching from Webster's dictionary and his life experiences, and it is the best I have seen.

> "Coaching is questioning and listening to help people articulate their future desired state of being, identify barriers to that desired state, build action steps for moving forward and stay on track over time. The end result is that the client has ownership and motivation to act on the plan and the odds of success are greatly increased"

Course Correct

The Greek philosopher, Heracleitus, said, "Good character is not formed in a week or a month. It is created little by little, day by day. Protracted and patient effort is needed to develop good character."[57] This is true for the "Intellectual framework" of your portfolio as well. But, Heraclitus also said, "The only constant, is change."

The three point triangle of changes loom over government programs like Medicare and Social Security. That's because the government, both federal and state, have basically three levers they can pull to restrict or enhance their programs. Once you meet criteria as an applicant, the benefits become an entitlement, which means they can't be taken away at the whim of a bureaucrat. They are required to be provided by law.

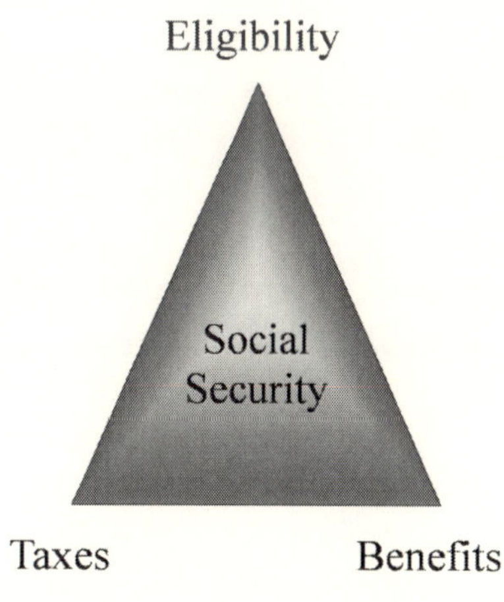

However, both federal and state statutes allow government agencies to control how new people come into the programs. Additionally, laws can be changed to tweak the criteria and the benefits provided. Finally, tax laws can be changed to encompass or charge more of the benefits received. Thus you need to monitor and pay attention to programs you know you will one day be using or are receiving now. It's not enough to just sign up and then go on cruise control. Forearmed with information is forewarned.

The first area they can attack is eligibility. They can change the barrier to entry by lowering the income requirement needed to get a benefit. They can change the eligibility age, for example, on Social Security the earliest benefit starts at sixty-two, but they could change that to sixty-five or some other age. Based on the past, governments usually make changes that can be "Sold" to the public. So they typically will not change the age eligibility because that affects everyone equally so they will attack the "Rich" and say they should not get a benefit because they do not need it. The problem lies not in the rhetoric, which is the symptom, the disease is always in the fine print and what you will usually find is that the "Rich" is you. Just because you do not feel rich does not mean the government does not classify you as rich. For example, the government started taxing social security benefits during the Clinton Administration. It was a tax on the "Rich." Rich was defined as a couple making over $34,000 a year. Does this seem rich to you? So when a politician try's to "Help" you, reach for your wallet first (to protect it) and then vote accordingly.

They will also raise taxes similar to the example that I just gave. Most tax increases are sold as something different in this country, but the bottom line is everyone pays for a tax increase. Just because someone else gets a tax does not mean it does not affect you. The whole economy is affected. For example, if I sell boats then I may be impacted by a tax on the wealthy because that tax may not affect the wealthy's lifestyle, but they may no longer want to buy new boats as often. This is an over simplistic example, but hopefully you can see the implications of taxes *on you* even if you thought the tax is not levied *against you*. The government will also "Tax" other ways. For example, the new popular "Tax" is to raise minimum wage. This ostensibly helps the lowest income, but it doesn't because when wages across the whole country go up, the businesses that pay the wage raise prices to offset the increased cost of doing business. So no one really gets a raise if everything is now more expensive. These are stealth ways to raise taxes. In one of many of life's great paradoxes, lowering taxes increases the revenue to government. In business if you want to generate more traffic, you lower prices and then more revenue comes in.

You make less per person, but more overall. Walmart has become the largest retailer on the planet in one generation with this strategy, but for some reason politicians ignore history (even though the lowering taxes strategy worked for John F. Kennedy (D) and Ronald Reagan (R)) and go with ideas that don't work, so keep an eye on both the overt tax and the covert tax.

The final option is they just cut benefits. This may seem obvious, but typically this happens covertly by taxing the benefits as they did with Social Security or changing the rules of how you can get to the benefits or rationing. I hope you see that these three tools the government uses are typically connected, they rarely use one at a time. The runaway spending the government is using to solve runaway government spending means benefits are likely to change with all three of the above strategies. So watch what they are doing so that you can adapt to the changes and try to be as self reliant as possible using the principles we have outlined here.

LONG-TERM DISABILITY INSURANCE OR LONG-TERM CARE

Long-term disability insurance helps replace your income if you are unable to work due to illness or injury. Many people consider this coverage a luxury, when in fact; it should be considered a necessity for those who don't have other financial resources they could tap in the event of an illness or injury. Even if you do have other financial resources, would you want to use them to pay your monthly bills? If you saved 5 percent of your income each year, a six-month disability would eat up ten years of savings!

Don't think it could happen to you? Although your chances of having a disability increase as you get older, illness and injury can happen at any age. Car accidents, sports injuries, back injuries, pregnancy, and disease are just a few examples. Men are particularly prone to injuries in the age bracket of thirty-five to fifty years of age. It is most damaging because men predominantly tend to be the major family's income-earner. Most believe they are careful enough, but broken legs, fractured hips, and injured backs top the list in incapacitation. You would think men would stop playing Thanksgiving football so much given the risk, right? That's not the case. It tends to be the household ladder. Falling from a height of one-story is more than enough to cause a severe injury, and every year hanging Christmas lights, cleaning gutters, standing on a house roof, or some other home repair project does the trick.

Ask yourself this question: could you live without your income for three months? Six months? A year? If the answer is no, you need disability insurance. Employers often offer this coverage via a payroll deduction, which may be tax-deductible.

Buy it, cover yourself, and protect your income source adequately.

Understand your Opponents

Your financial opponents can be overt or subtle.

Opponents from Within (Family and Friends)

Not everyone needs to know your budget and financial plan. But the people who rely on you; your spouse, partner, and family need to know what you are doing. Many folks make a critical mistake in this issue. Their view can be, as long as they have it under control, no one else needs know. There's also the camp that says, "I'm the one that earned it, so therefore I'm the one who decides how to use it." Both are incorrect. If you take on the responsibility of providing a living for someone else, they have a right to know how they are being taken care. Remember, you voluntarily got married, involved, or had children. No one forced you into that choice. Financial awareness is part of the package.

That said, your parents, your parent-in-laws, the neighbors, your third cousin removed, and the post office don't need to know your plans. Again, the people who rely on you are the critical audience.

Critical Audience: Your Spouse or Partner

If you want to maintain a good relationship with your spouse or partner in the long-term, you need to communicate regularly on your finances. Part of communication means also being forthright about financial issues that you share. Half of today's marital issues involve some sort of financial issue that has come between the couple.

To do this right, your spouse or partner needs to be involved in all aspects. This is tougher than it sounds. Prior to being in a relationship you had your own financial life. You had your own checking, credit card, credit history, spending trends, and income. Now when you join with someone else, you are sharing all the good and bad financial aspects of each other. That includes your habits and your approach to budgeting.

Some people don't like to share this kind of information. Some try to keep their separate financial lives and not coexist financially. This may work for a while, but ultimately the day will come when the management of your resources and spending comes down to whether you trust your partner or not. If you can't trust that person, it's really going to bring into question the future of your relationships.

If you have a spouse or partner that works against your financial plan, you in essence have an enemy in your house. Don't confuse this with advice to get divorced; that's not what I mean. You have someone who is working in the opposite direction of where your plan needs to go. You save, they spend. You study; they go with the latest trend. You question pros and cons; they throw risk to the wind. If you're in this kind of situation, you're going to need to lay down ground rules you both can live on. Otherwise, your financial plan is going to get mucked up real quick. Why? Because you want competing goals from it. Plans work best when the players agree on the same end desired result. How can you plan a meal you will both enjoy if one wants Asian food and the other Mexican food? Just like in a situation where there is dissent in other areas of a relationship, you may want to seek help from an outside perspective, someone who can coach you through the process of meeting in the middle.

Opponents on the Outside (Everyone Wants your Money)

You become quite a popular person as retirement nears and if you have a retirement account, but not for the reasons you think. Sorry to disappoint your ego. A few of us may have charisma, but most of us have something else people want instead: money.

The good news is you have been taught how to identify them! (See the Business Models section)

FINANCIAL ADVISORS

Your financial advisor, if you find the right kind, is there to help you. To do that, he or she is going to need to see your entire financial picture. That means the advisor will need to cover everything from your goals, to your budget, to your spending, to your taxes.

It may seem overwhelming to have someone you only know through a contract to go poking around in your financial history and files. In this modern day when we are so concern with identity theft and privacy, this is a scary thing. Very few people are going to want to provide *everything* about them, financially.

For a financial advisor to really do their job, they must see your entire picture. Otherwise, they will make assumptions in their analysis that don't really apply to your financial life.

The bottom line is you are paying for the advice provided. The advice is contingent upon the information provided. This relationship falls into the old computer adage:

> *Garbage in, garbage out.*

If you don't want to be fully honest with your advisor, then don't waste your money on a financial advisor. If you want good, objective advice to plan with, then you need to be completely honest with your advisor. You will want to see this relationship the same way you see the relationship with your doctor. What they don't know about one of your habits, like smoking, will have a big impact on the overall discussion of your health.

Health Costs and Other Boondoggles to Avoid Near Retirement

Some of the things that we consider to be unexpected can be anticipated and prepared for and inoculated against.

The Health Gap before Medicare—Retiring Too Soon

Money isn't the only reason retirees head back to work. They are also in search of affordable health insurance. A lot of folks simply don't realize the expense until they've made the wrong decision. After a need for money, the need for health benefits was the number-two reason preretirees surveyed by AARP said they would work in retirement.

The most at risk are lower net-worth individuals who can't afford individual health insurance policies, but who retire before qualifying for Medicare. People who can't realistically foot the bill for health insurance should put off retirement at least until they turn 631/2.

What makes that the magical age? The Consolidated Omnibus Reconciliation Act (COBRA) does. COBRA gives people who have retired, resigned or been laid off the right to keep group health insurance for up to eighteen months. If you retire at sixty-three-and-a-half you can continue on your former employer's COBRA policy until Medicare kicks in at sixty-five.

Federal law requires most employers who have twenty or more workers to offer COBRA benefits (church plans are exempt). Firms with fewer than twenty employees may be subject to COBRA-like requirements under state law.

In most circumstances, you can buy up to eighteen months of continuing coverage. Some states let you keep your benefits longer. Also death, divorce or a legal separation from a spouse may trigger a longer benefit period. Entitlement to Medicare may also qualify your dependents for extended COBRA benefits once you lose health care coverage at work (usually up to thirty-six months). Be prepared for "Sticker shock" COBRA usually expensive.

Once you reach sixty-five you qualify for Medicare, the health insurance offered by the federal government (Medicare is also available to younger people with disabilities). If you are getting social security benefits or railroad retirement benefits, you are automatically signed up for Medicare. If not, you can sign up by calling or visiting your local Social Security Administration office.

But keep a close eye on the calendar. There are very specific times when you can sign up for the government coverage: three months before your sixty-fifth birthday, the month of your birthday or the three months after your birthday. It's best to sign up before your birthday.

When you sign up, you are enrolled in Medicare Part A, which covers hospital bills. Most people don't pay a monthly premium for Part A. However, if you want coverage for doctors' visits, you will have to sign up for Part B. The current standard premium for Part B is $96.40; however the amount adjusts yearly depending on the CPI (Consumer Price Index). If you wait to sign up for Part B, your premium could go up 10 percent for each year you could have had Part B coverage.

You can also choose to supplement Medicare to fill gaps in coverage. So-called "Medigap" policies are offered through the private sector. To qualify for a Medigap policy, you must be enrolled in Part A and B. You have a six-month window after signing up for Part B to enroll in Medigap. If you don't sign up during this period, you could be denied coverage or charged more for a Medigap policy.

Although COBRA is expensive and Medicare has its shortcomings, they are a sure thing. You can't be turned down for an individual policy or pay higher premiums if you have health problems. That's why finding insurance on your own can be so daunting.

If you've been covered continuously by a group plan for at least eighteen months and have used up your COBRA or similar state-continuation benefit, you have the right under federal law to buy the policy of your choice from a company selling individual health insurance, and your coverage must be effective immediately. But if there are gaps in your coverage, you lose this right.

The Sucker Punch—Employment Change

You've got your retirement lined up, you're maybe three to five years out from the final day, you're anticipating all the things you want to do, and then you get the sucker punch. The market melts down, your employer is on the ropes, and more importantly your job is at risk.

This is probably the worst scenario that can happen to one's planning so close to retirement because if you don't have the right safety net in place, you could find yourself sapping all your hard-earned savings just to pay your bills if unemployed. Why? The cold, hard truth is that experienced, senior employees cost a lot of money. Companies, in their short-sightedness, cut expensive employees first for short-term savings in downturns. Payroll is the most easily liquidated expense in a business.

If you are one of the lucky to see this coming, make sure to have put in place the following steps in your planning with your financial coach:[58]

- Build a substantial savings account today so you will be OK if you are laid off.
- Do not—repeat, do not—go without health insurance. Medical expenses in later age are the fastest consumer of savings with out-of-pocket charges. Shop for private health insurance if you are laid off; it is often less expensive than COBRA.
- Purchase an affordable term life insurance policy if anyone is dependent on your income and make sure you have all your estate-planning documents in order.
- Get out of all forms of debt.

The best way to protect your family is to know that you will still be able to pay the bills while you look for a new job. Because of the weak economy, that could take longer than you may think.

Now let's say you instead fall into the group that is to be laid off. If you're still fortunate, you will be part of a surplus process. This gives you some time before the actual pink slip hits. Some companies in fact offer an early severance and you may be able to negotiate for an even bigger package, depending on your situation. If you know termination is inevitable, don't throw the offer away; instead, leverage it for more than or as much as you can get. It may be enough to get you to your original retirement date, at which time your plan kicks back in and you can move forward without any problems.

If however, your termination is more abrupt, i.e., it's Wednesday and the pink slips arrive in two weeks on Friday (terminations, discipline, and demotions always happen at the end of the week under some belief that people's anger will go away over the weekend but human nature has repeatedly proven that theory false), then your response plan has to be more immediate. You want to start your job hunt right now—while you still have your current job. Network like crazy, show up at industry conferences, and take a look at job postings in your field. If there is any specific skill mentioned that you are not up to speed on, get yourself schooled on it ASAP. In a slow economy, employers won't hire someone who meets 80 percent of their needs; they have such a large pool to choose from that they can find the person who meets 100 percent of their needs. Make sure that person is you.[59]

A new job hunt may mean taking a pay cut. Yes, it stinks. You're worth more. But put aside your ego for a moment. Your goal is to keep your noble purpose and financial plan on track. Earning money avoids deterioration of your assets and gains so far. Besides, after the stress subsides, you might like the career change. Many do, believe it or not. Again, remember your purpose; don't fixate on the immediate moment.

Making sure that inheritance happens

Plan for the inevitable time when you will no longer be here.

Legacy Planning

Movies are one of the most popular forms of entertainment. This is for good reason. There are a huge variety of movies and hundreds of movies are released every year. Some movies you forget immediately and yet others are so awful or good that you can't forget. Some inspire you to do something. After seeing the movie, American Flyers, a movie about cycling, many people went out and bought a bike and started training for the Tour de France! Movies that inspire are rare and even more uncommon are movies that change lives. Lawrence of Arabia inspired many and changed the lives of a few. Stephen Spielberg has attributed this movie to changing the course of his life.

What makes a movie better than others? Is it the story itself or is it the ending? The case can be made for either, but most would agree the ending is of paramount importance. The ending makes the movie. A good story needs to have the exclamation point of a good ending. Life is like a movie. Life needs a good ending.

Joe Robbie's life was an American success story. He was a successful entrepreneur and cofounder of the Miami Dolphins, a franchise that turned into one of the highest profile and most lucrative teams in professional football. During his span as owner, Joe Robbie and Coach Don Shula led the Dolphins to an unfathomable perfect season, won two Super Bowls (1973 and 1974) and built the $115 million

Joe Robbie Stadium. At the time, unlike any other open-air facility, Joe Robbie Stadium was the first to be constructed entirely with private funds.

Like many owners of family-run businesses, it was Robbie's dream to have his family follow in his footsteps when he was gone. Unfortunately, Robbie never planned to deal with estate taxes. He died on January 7, 1990. Through the marriage deduction, he passed to his wife the illustrious franchise and the stadium which bore his name. Unfortunately, his wife passed away soon thereafter, and due to a lack of planning, a staggering estate bill estimated at $47 million was left behind. Differing views amongst his nine children only exacerbated the situation and forced the cash-poor family to sell Robbie's legacy he had worked so hard to build. In 1994, the family sold both the team and the stadium for a total of $138 million. At that time, the sale price, even after estate taxes, was impressive. Today, many would argue that the Dolphins and the stadium might be worth twice as much. More important, however, Robbie's intentions were defeated; his family was removed from the success he worked so hard to build.

You may not have been as fortunate, in your wealth, as Joe Robbie, but you may share his ending. You can avoid leaving a shadow over your life by designing your legacy. A legacy that outlives you, a legacy that takes your values and wishes and sends them like a time capsule onto the subsequent generations.

Contrast Joe Robbie's story with that of Sam Walton who left over twenty-five billion to his heirs and not a dime was paid in estate taxes. Most people miss the second part of this statement and only think, "I don't have twenty-five billion dollars." The point that should not be missed is his heirs paid no estate taxes. Sam Walton left a legacy, even if it was just keeping his wealth in the hands of his family and not the government. So what makes Sam different than Joe? It can be summed up in one word, planning.

Untold millions of dollars are unnecessarily lost to estate taxes because of the dreaded "P" word—procrastination. It takes a highly motivated individual to invest their time and energy into planning something that will benefit others, especially when you consider that the person won't be around to see the results of his or her hard work.

The idea that someone cannot see the results of their hard work is the down fall of estate planning. Estate planning is about assets and money. Legacy planning is about people, dreams and values. Os Guinness said in his book, *The Call,* "As modern people, we are all on a search for significance. We desire to make a difference. We long to leave a legacy. We yearn, as Ralph Waldo Emerson put it, 'To leave the world a bit better.'"[60]

Legacy planning does this and it needs estate planning because dreams need to be funded. Stephen Covey in his bestselling book, *Seven Habits of Highly Successful People*, talks about "Keeping the end in mind." This is what Sam Walton did. He thought ahead and determined that his money was better left to his family than to his government. Judging by Walmart and Sam's Club's growth after he died, he was right, unless you think the government could have done a better job of using those resources.

Amelia Pohl, the primary author of several state specific estate planning books titled, *Guiding Those Left Behind In . . .*, as well as, *When Someone Dies In . . .*, said: "If you think that only wealthy people need to prepare an estate plan, you are mistaken. Each year, heirs of relatively modest estates spend thousands of dollars to settle an estate. A bit of planning could have eliminated most, if not all, of the hassle and cost suffered by these families."

Don't be the New England Patriots football team. They were undefeated the entire season except one minute. They did everything right, but that one minute changed everything.

Keep the end in mind. Develop your legacy, your ending, than your personal movie and story will be great.

Probate

I am not an attorney so before I start explaining the ingredients that can be used for a good Legacy Plan, let me throw out a disclaimer. I am not a lawyer and you will need one to know exactly what documents you will need for your specific situation. Also, I will attempt to discuss these legal issues without being boring. I will start with probate.

The disposition of someone's estate is handled through a court process called probate. Probate is the Latin word for "Prove the will." It specifically resolves all claims and distributes the deceased person's property under the valid will. Probate is a service that a Surrogate Court provides to confirm the validity of a deceased person's will. Once a will has been probated by the court, everyone can rely on its authenticity. Probate protects the instructions of the deceased, confirms the executor as the personal representative of the estate, protects the interests of family members who may have claims against the estate, and protects the executor against claims and lawsuits. Probate can be a hassle for the survivors. There are numerous filings and notices, and sometimes delays occasioned by the necessity of getting Court approval for so many things. Probate can also be very costly. Probate is basically suing yourself with your own money after you died. If that statement doesn't make you want to minimize the impact of dying you can skip this section.

Wills, Trusts, and Life Insurance

One of the easiest ways to limit the costs of probate is with a will.

A will or testament is a document by which a person (the testator) regulates the rights of others over his or her property or family after death. Everybody needs a will. If you do nothing else, at least have this in place. No matter your age or what you do, your will is the device that tells where to direct your assets. This is a simple set of instructions that helps the Probate Court follow your wishes, otherwise you leave it to state laws.

Believe it or not, however, most property today passes outside of a will. In other words, the existing will is overridden. For example, if you own a home jointly with a spouse and one of you dies, the house goes to the surviving spouse who is the joint owner, regardless of what your will says. It passes by operation of law and supersedes any conflicting provision of your will. The same is true of property that passes by beneficiary designation, such as an IRA, a company retirement account, or an insurance policy. They have assigned destinations and are transferred according to the designated beneficiary form, not the will. The beneficiary form controls the distribution of the money in those accounts. It is, in effect, the will for your IRA that guarantees the stretch option for your beneficiaries.[61]

IRA expert, Ed Slott says, "The last thing you want is your IRA to pass to your estate as a beneficiary. Once the IRA is paid to the estate, there cannot be a designated beneficiary on your IRA, which means no beneficiary which means no stretch option for your heirs."[62]

THE LIVING TRUST/REVOCABLE TRUST

In the United States, a living trust refers to a trust that may be revocable by the trust creator or settlor (known by the IRS as the Grantor). Living trusts are often used because they may allow assets to be passed to heirs without going through the process of probate. Avoiding probate will normally save substantial costs (the probate courts, in some states, charge a fee based on a percentage net worth of the deceased), time, and maintain privacy (the probate records are available to the public, while distribution through a trust is private).

Living trusts also can be utilized to plan for unforeseen circumstances such as incapacity or disability. The grantor/ settlor may also serve as a trustee or cotrustee. In the case where two or more cotrustees serve, the trust instrument may provide that either trustee may act alone on behalf of the trust or require both cotrustees to act/sign. The trust instrument may also provide that the other cotrustee shall act as sole trustee if the grantor becomes incompetent and is unable to continue administering the trust.

Despite the advantages, there are also some negative aspects to a living trust in the United States. Beneficiaries do not save on federal estate or state inheritance taxes. Setting up a trust may be expensive, and the expense is immediate, not delayed till after the grantor's death. A Living Trust can be a hassle to keep up with, during life. However, in the long run depending on the circumstances, the expense is usually substantially less to set up a trust and the estate administration is generally much faster when compared to probate.

Living trusts can be used as an alternative to a will. With a living trust, you transfer (or retitle) property to a trust while you are alive but maintain control of your assets by naming yourself the trustee. You can amend this trust easily throughout your lifetime; when you die, the trust will be distributed according to specifications you lay out in the trust agreement. The cost to set one up varies, but is usually between $750 to $3,000, depending on your details and complexity. And it allows your loved ones to steer clear of the costs and hassles of probate.

Irrevocable Trust

These trusts provide more stringent control on assets after you die. Property won't be placed in trust until after your death; you can stipulate exactly how you want your money managed and name a trustee—typically a relative, close friend or lawyer, to execute your instructions. Various types can meet your needs including:[63]

- Credit shelter trust—also known as an AB or bypass trust, you write an amount equal to the estate tax exemption, specify how you want the trust to use those assets, and then pass the remainder to your spouse. This doubles the exemption allowed because then your surviving spouse can use his or her exemption subsequent to yours.
- Generation-skipping trust—also known as a dynasty trust. There are some that believe Congress will eliminate this trust.
- Qualified personal residence trust (QPRT)—used for shielding a house or vacation home from estate taxes, you can put it in a QPRT, which allows you give away your home, generally to your children, while you keep control of it over a period that you can stipulate, usually five to fifteen years. This allows you to take the value of your home out of your estate that passes on. One problem, if you die before the trust runs out, your home will be included in your estate at its fair market value.
- Qualified terminable interest property trust (QTIP)—this trust allows you to direct specific assets to specific relatives. Your spouse gets the income from the assets in the trust when you die, and then the designated beneficiaries get the principal when your spouse dies. This is very effective for people who have divorced and remarried.

THE LIFE INSURANCE TRUST (ILIT)

A life insurance trust is an irrevocable, nonamendable trust that is both the owner and beneficiary of one or more life insurance policies. Upon the death of the insured, the Trustee invests the insurance proceeds and administers the trust for one or more beneficiaries. If the trust owns insurance on the life of a married person, the noninsured spouse and children are often beneficiaries of the insurance trust. If the trust owns "Second to die" or survivorship insurance, which only pays when both spouses are deceased, only the children would be beneficiaries of the insurance trust.

In the United States, proper ownership of life insurance is important if the insurance proceeds are to escape federal estate taxation. If the policy is owned by the insured, the proceeds will be subject to estate tax. (This assumes that the aggregate value of the estate plus the life insurance is large enough to be subject to estate taxes.) To avoid estate taxation, some insurers name a child, spouse, or other beneficiary as the owner of the policy.

There are, however, two drawbacks to having insurance proceeds paid outright to a child, spouse, or other beneficiary.

Doing so may be inconsistent with the insured's wishes or the best interests of the beneficiary, who might be a minor or lacking in financial sophistication and unable to invest the proceeds wisely.

The insurance proceeds will be included in the beneficiary's taxable estate at his or her subsequent death. If the proceeds are used to pay the insured's estate taxes, it would at first appear that the proceeds could not be on hand to be taxed at the beneficiary's subsequent death. However, using insurance proceeds to pay the insured's estate taxes, effectively increases the beneficiary's estate since the beneficiary will not have to sell inherited assets to pay such taxes.

The solution to both drawbacks is usually an irrevocable life insurance trust. But, once again get help from someone that knows what they are doing. The final tool ingredient you need to consider in your document mix is the IRA Inheritance Trust.

IRA Inheritance Trusts

An IRA Inheritance Trust does what a trust does but is for an IRA. As more "Baby boomers" are retiring and rolling over large 401(k) and other retirement plans to IRAs, proper tax and estate planning for IRAs have become increasingly important.

When an IRA owner becomes seventy-and-a-half years old, he or she must soon begin to take required minimum withdrawals (RMDs) and pay federal and state income taxes on those withdrawals at his or her highest rate brackets (unless the IRA is a Roth, in which case the withdrawals may be income tax-free).

Effective January 1, 2003, the IRS changed its RMD rules, allowing a nonspouse beneficiary (for example, a child) to take or "Stretch-out" the taxable RMDs over a much longer period, using his or her own life expectancy rather than the shorter life expectancy of the original IRA owner (the parent). This means that money inside an inherited IRA may now compound much longer, tax-deferred.

For example, let's take a child age forty-five (at the time of his parent's death) who inherits a $200,000 IRA and withdraws only RMDs. If the IRA grows, from both income and principal appreciation, at the rate of 6 percent a year, then thirty years later when the child is age seventy-five, the child will have taken over $400,000 in RMDs and still have almost $300,000 left in the IRA to use over his or her later years or pass down to his or her children (the original IRA owner's grandchildren).

To sum it up, the original $200,000 inherited IRA became worth over $700,000 to that family! (And that doesn't include the future value of the RMDs if they're placed into an investment account). If we assume the IRA will be worth over $200,000 when the owner passes, or will earn a higher rate of annual return, or will go to a younger beneficiary, that IRA may eventually be worth well over $1 Million!

In other words, IRAs may now be a huge part of a family's financial future, perhaps for generations—and now large

IRAs require a higher level of tax and estate planning—which you can look into with a qualified estate planning attorney that is currently implementing this process.

Many IRA owners and their professional advisors "Assume" that the IRA beneficiaries will make the right "Stretch-out" decisions, or at least seek the advisor's help before they take withdrawals. Unfortunately, that is often not the case when the IRA owner dies.

The beneficiaries are not prohibited from withdrawing more than the RMDs and may instead decide to cash out the IRA earlier than required, blowing the stretch-out. This happens because beneficiaries are:

- Not aware of the RMD rules and their choices.
- See themselves listed as beneficiaries on an account and immediately transfer it into their own names.
- Go to the custodian asking what to do, are given a check and then immediately cash and deposit it in their own accounts.
- Do what they think (wrongly) is a tax-free rollover to their own IRAs.
- Just can't wait to get their hands on the IRA money or are influenced by a spouse or some other third-party to grab and spend it!

Yanking the IRA money out too quickly—resulting in what we call the "blowout"—may force a family to pay all the taxes up front and lose over one-third of the IRA's future value—literally throwing away hundreds of thousands of dollars, or even millions!

Let's assume the IRA beneficiary will properly do the RMD "Stretch-out" and pay the taxes gradually over his or her lifetime. A lot can still go wrong.

When a beneficiary receives an inheritance directly, as is the case when an individual is named directly as the beneficiary of an IRA, his or her inheritance can then be exposed to a number of significant problems:

- The wrong people may later inherit the IRA (the child, as initial beneficiary, could name his or her spouse as next beneficiary and that spouse's next husband or wife or that spouse's children of another marriage could inherit the account!)
- The beneficiary, his or her spouse or children may have poor spending habits (be "Spendthrifts!").
- The beneficiary may lack good money management/investment skills.
- A beneficiary's spouse may take some or all of the IRA in a DIVORCE! (The income tax laws, allowing an IRA transfer in a divorce to be tax-free, actually encourage the spouse to grab it, and keep in mind the statistical chance of a divorce is now over 50 percent!).
- If the beneficiary is too young, elderly or disabled, he or she may not be able to properly manage his or her own affairs—without unwanted court intervention.
- A beneficiary who now or later in life receives needs-based government benefits (like Medicaid nursing care benefits or supplemental disability income) may not qualify for or lose those benefits.

In most states (including California), an IRA is not creditor protected and can be grabbed in a lawsuit, even a bogus one that forces a beneficiary to settle.

In other words, an inherited IRA not only needs to take advantage of "Stretch-out," but needs protection too—the kind that a trust can provide.

In its RMD regulations and previous rulings, the IRS had made it very difficult for an IRA inherited through a trust to both qualify for maximum tax "Stretch-out" using each primary beneficiary's own life expectancy and also achieve the higher level of asset protection afforded by a trust that may accumulate the RMDs and hold them for future distribution. Generally, one benefit had to be traded off for the other.

The new IRA Inheritance Trust now permits the IRA owner and his or her family to enjoy maximum “Stretch-out” and protection benefits at the same time. The protective features of this trust have previously been tested and proven over many years of court decisions. And now, in September 2005, the IRS approved the income tax “Stretch-out” feature as well. This new standalone IRA beneficiary trust is not the “Garden variety” that has existed for some time, but rather represents a huge breakthrough. The IRA Inheritance Trust is the most advanced “Next generation” trust that solves many earlier, tricky drafting problems associated with maximizing both the stretch-out and protection benefits.

Effective January 1, 2007, the Pension Protection Act (PPA) significantly widened the application of the IRA Inheritance Trust to people who may never have considered this valuable planning tool before. For anyone who has IRAs (including those owned by his or her spouse) and/or 401(k) or other retirement plans that total over $200,000—this IRA Inheritance Trust is virtually a “No brainer” decision.

Simply stated, the income tax reduction and asset protection planning that this trust now provides may save a million dollars or more for that IRA owner’s (or retirement plan participant’s) family!

Previously, this Trust had no application to a company retirement plan—401(k), 403a, 403(b), 457, pension or profit-sharing plan, etc.-unless and until the worker/participant reached normal retirement age and took an “In service” distribution or retired, and then rolled over the company plan into an IRA. The reason why is that company plans’ own rules usually forced a nonspouse beneficiary to take the entire taxable distribution in one to five years, overriding the income tax “Stretch-out” rules available to IRAs.

Now, if someone has more than $150,000 in company plans, is still working but has not reached normal retirement age, or has retired but left these moneys in the company plan, this plan participant can take advantage of the stretch-out and protection benefits for his or her family available through the IRA Inheritance Trust.

The PPA permits nonspouse beneficiaries of company plans, or a Trust established on the beneficiaries' behalf, to do a rollover into an "Inherited IRA" after the plan participant passes away. In other words, a company plan participant can set up the IRA Inheritance Trust® now, make it the beneficiary of the plan and let the IRA rollover occur later!

If you haven't seriously considered the IRA Inheritance Trust because you are still working or have retired but still have money in a company retirement plan, you definitely need to look into it right away!

Remember the main points of how the IRA Inheritance Trust works and provides protection of undistributed balance—even for company plans and Roth IRAs:

- Proper distribution to intended beneficiaries
- Protection against the spendthrift
- Professional money management
- Divorce protection
- Protection for minors
- Protection for elderly or disabled
- Government benefits protection
- Lawsuit, creditor, and bankruptcy protection
- Minimized future estate taxes

LIFE INSURANCE POLICIES

A life insurance policy is one that basically agrees to pay a lump sum of money to a designated beneficiary in the instance that you die. You pay monthly or quarterly premiums to the insurance company to keep the policy in place and at a certain payout value. The idea is to make sure your beneficiaries are financially taken care of if you die unexpectedly. Policy costs are based on your health, age, and potential health risks. They come in limited-term policies (usually a number of years specific, i.e., ten years, twenty years, etc.) and whole life, which tends to be more expensive since they offer longer protection.

Life Insurance is a bet. It says that if something goes wrong in a particular way, an insurance company will pay you a sum of money to help correct that problem. The insurance company is betting that that particular event will not occur. And if it doesn't, then the monthly premium you pay to the insurance company is pure profit for them. However, if the particular event does occur, then the insurance company loses. Insurance companies have a vested interest to make sure when a loss does occur; it is covered in the contract with the insured.

Once again I quote Ed Slott, CPA, from his book, *The Retirement Savings Time Bomb . . . and How to Defuse It.* "You should have enough life insurance to cover the taxes and other expenses that must be paid on your estate after you're gone. To do that, you will need to know the balance in your account at the time of your death, which means, you will have to project that balance. You cannot go by today's market or values—because if you have an IRA that's worth, say, $1 million right now and you are only sixty years old, that IRA could easily be worth $5 million or more over the long-term, given today's long life expectancies.

A good rule of thumb is to buy enough life insurance to cover at least 50 percent of the project value of your estate at your death. It's good to buy a lot now if young. When you and your account grow older (and fatter), not only will purchasing more life insurance become an increasingly expensive proposition, but if your health deteriorates you make become uninsurable."[64]

For you, the consumer developing a budget, insurance is worth it if you have something to protect. This would include your ability to earn income, your car, your family, your home, or maybe particular valuables. In any case, losing these things can be a huge financial bite to replace. Insurance mitigates this loss with a small monthly cost. When you have a lot riding on making sure something bad doesn't happen to your family or home, the cost of an insurance plan can seem pretty small in comparison. But you need to be able to afford it. That depends on how much insurance you need.

How much life insurance do you need? Well, you're actually the one best able to answer that question. Ignore blanket formulas that suggest you need something like five to ten times your annual income. Each person's situation is different. Look at insurance not as a lottery-like payoff, but as filling a specific need. If you're insuring your own life, you need to think about the financial impact of your demise on your family.

Take out a pen and paper and do the following:

- List yourself and the members of your family.
- List how much money comes in from various sources.
- List how much various people need each year.
- Think about how these numbers will change over time.
- Think about the contributions you would have been making over the years to any college funds or to your retirement nest egg. You'll want your insurance policy to fill those gaps.
- Are you also supporting your mother-in-law? If so, you'll want to make sure she isn't left in the lurch should you get run over by a bus.
- You also have to consider additional expenses your spouse will face as a single parent. With two toddlers or an aging parent to support, for example, will he or she be able to pay for the extra child care help, maybe get a lawn-care service for the house, afford daytime

help for the mother-in-law, and still be able to work if you die? If not, you need insurance to cover your spouse's lost income and the added expenses he or she will face.

If your kids' future educational costs are already covered and your mother-in-law has sufficient insurance of her own, you may not need very much in the way of insurance. And if you're single with no dependents, you may not need any at all. If you die, you will be missed, but your income stream won't. Spend some time thinking about how much coverage you need to protect your loved ones from financial hardships posed by your death. You may need a lot of coverage now, and much less a few years down the road.[65]

If you need insurance for a limited time-say, before you start working or while you're between jobs-consider buying a short-term health plan, which lasts from one to six months. If you're going to need insurance indefinitely-say, because you are or expect to be self-employed—it makes sense to buy an individual health policy that has a high deductible. You'll have to pay that much out of pocket before the insurance kicks in, but you'll be covered in case of that broken leg.

In return for the high deductible, your premiums will be considerably lower and more affordable. If the deductible is at least $1,050 in 2006, you will be eligible to contribute pretax money to a health savings account, which you can use to pay for out-of-pocket medical bills. For help finding a policy, go to eHealthInsurance.com, or search for an insurance agent through the National Association of Health Underwriters at: *www.nahu.org*

Life insurance is necessary if you have dependents who will suffer financially if you die (children, for example). If you have no financial dependents, it's probably not necessary, although many people also use insurance as part of their estate planning and cash accumulation regardless of their dependent status.

If you plan to buy insurance other than term insurance provided by your employer, you should educate yourself about the pros and cons of term, whole life, and other types of insurance. In this case you absolutely would need to look for one of the business models we have already talked about because if you don't you are likely to be sold a lot of premium (which is what the commission is paid on) not life insurance. Like the tools in your kitchen, that are far more effective in the hands of a professional chef who is making something specifically for you, Life Insurance needs to be handled by someone not selling it, but using it to accomplish your specific needs.

Life insurance money is already income-tax-free, but if you're not careful, it will be subject to estate tax. You should set up the policy, so that it is not included as an asset of your estate. If it is included, its value is effectively cut in half. If you own the policy when you die, it's part of your estate and Uncle Sam gets the 49 percent via estate tax. Unfortunately, this is how most people set up life insurance. Instead, your beneficiaries should own the policy and can pay premiums from money you gift them. This can be set up automatically via an irrevocable life insurance trust (ILIT). The trust owns the policy and the trustee pays the premium from money deposited into the trust. The main point is not to own the policy when you die. Thus all the proceeds are then excluded from the estate.[66]

I will give you an example of how one client we will call Dan, used trusts and life insurance to pass his wealth and his legacy at the same time. Dan would have been considered by most to be well past his retirement years. But, he did not want to sell his $3 million construction businesses that he started in his garage. Due to the Federal and State tax codes of where he lived he would have had to give away over 50 percent of his business proceeds in taxes. Because of this, he just kept working. Dan was eventually able to solve this onerous tax problem with trusts and life insurance. He set up a charitable remainder trust (CRT) in which his church was the named owner and he was trustee. He sold the business and paid no taxes since it was technically owned by the church a nonprofit organization. Since he had just “Given” the church a $3,000,000 business, he began to distribute an income to himself tax-free (he had a $3,000,000 charitable donation offset). He bought a $3,000,000 life insurance policy paid for by the CRT that would go into an individual life insurance trust (ILIT) when he died, which was outside of the estate. If he died earlier than expected, the church got whatever was left in the CRT and his three kids got one million dollars each.

But, he did not stop there. He did not want the kids to each inherit $1,000,000 and then irresponsibly waste his life’s work. Also, this kind of wealth can destroy children, not help them. He knew this so he built in two controversial (to many, but the money was his) rules. The first was that if his daughters got pregnant before marriage and/or his son got a girl pregnant before marriage they would get nothing and there portion would be given to charity. Second, and this is the one I thought showed incredible foresight and wisdom, was that his kids could only access the money in the trust based on what they earned. For example, if the child wanted to make $20,000 a year working at an entry level job, he wanted his wealth to make their life easier so the trust would match the $20,000. If the child worked hard and took risks and they were able to make $100,000 a year then the trust would match them until their 1/3 of the inheritance had been fully paid out.

His goal was to incentivize his kids so that they could better realize their full potential and at the same time not enable and/or discourage the self-destructive behavior. He did not just leave money, he left a legacy. Although the laws are not the same as they were back then, many of the same types of things can be done today with good legacy planning.

Here is the reality.[67]

- You will die
- You will take nothing with you
- You will probably die at a time, you do not anticipate
- Someone else will get your "Stuff"
- You can only decide before you die who gets your "Stuff" after you die

If you don't decide before you die, someone you may not know, you may not like, and may not believe what you believe, will decide for you where all your "Stuff" goes after you die. If this is not bad enough, if you have enough "Stuff" you may create a legacy where you are hated or where people are fighting over what you should have handled while you were alive.

I have a client whose husband never bothered to change beneficiaries so the ex-wife got everything and she was left destitute. Another man left his wife destitute and two daughters from a previous marriage wealthy. Another woman's husband was counting on his parent's money for his retirement. The problem is that he "Left" his wife of forty years when he died of a heart attack. His mother (her mother-in-law) immediately changed her will and sent her considerable fortune to her grandkids instead, who were in there mid-1930s. The grandson was living with my client who was scraping by supporting herself and her alcoholic son (the grandson) who just inherited a fortune.

I had two women in the same year that both had husbands that had chosen me as their financial advisor. One in his early 1950s died suddenly the other in his late 1970s died of cancer. Neither woman implemented my suggestions. Both have paid for those mistakes. I can go on for pages, but do you see a pattern? Women get hit the hardest by bad legacy planning.

The *facts* are . . . [68]

- 80 percent of women will experience widowhood
- The average age widow in 2000 was fifty-five
- 80 percent of widows now in poverty were not in poverty before their husband died
- Life expectancy of a widow is a minimum of eighteen years

The saying the knowledge is power is not true, because know the stories and the statistics don't matter if you don't do something about it, now!

ELDER ABUSE AND CON ARTISTS

Elder abuse is a general term used to describe certain types of harm to older adults. Other terms commonly used include: "Senior abuse," "Abuse in later life," "Abuse of older adults," "Abuse or older women" and "Abuse of older men."

One of the more commonly accepted definitions of elder abuse is "A single, or repeated act, or lack of appropriate action, occurring within any relationship where there is an expectation of trust, which causes harm or distress to an older person."

The core feature of this definition is that it focuses on harms where there is "expectation of trust" of the older person toward their abuser. Thus it includes harms by people the older person knows or with whom they have a relationship, such as a spouse, partner, or family member, a friend or neighbor, or people that the older person relies on for services. Many forms of elder abuse are recognized as types of domestic violence or family violence.

The term elder abuse does not include general criminal activity against older persons, such as "muggings" in the street or "distraction burglary," where a stranger distracts an older person at the doorstep while another person enters the property to steal.

Most elder abuse usually happens without any violence. Instead, the intent is to steal money and valuables, either over time or through a tweaking of legal documents to get power of attorney. If successful, then the elderly person's accounts are emptied systematically.

Take the example of Peter. Peter grew up in Germany, lived through two world wars, saw Europe destroyed and reconstructed through the Marshall Plan and saw his own career as a chemist blossom. In the heyday of German industrialization, Peter took his chemist degree and leveraged it into a career in petroleum refining. He shot up the ranks and eventually became a CEO of a German refinery. Peter spent years amassing his fortune, putting his money into property, market instruments, savings, and various other pots. Peter also had three sons, each of which had children and they in turn produced Peter's great grandchildren. In his later years, he made sure to establish the means for each generation to do better than he did starting out, with his goal that they all should have the chance of a good education and the chance to go farther than he did in life.

Peter also had the fortune, or misfortune, to grow to a long one hundred years of age. With his sons living great distances from him, his wife now passed on, and no relatives nearby, Peter relied on help to keep him company, provide him transportation, and provide him with medical assistance. Similar to his family, Peter took care of his provider, a former office friend who helped him with his needs. Unknowingly, the friend was also figuring out just how well off Peter still was financially.

Despite already having set aside a pension for her assistance to the tune of approximately $675,000, and the stipend she received from the German government being a caretaker of a senior citizen, Peter's caretaker still went about changing his last will and getting his signature to empty Peter's bank accounts. When Peter passed away, his sons found the caretaker long gone and nothing left in his estate to pass on.

Peter's mistake was, trusting his friend as a caretaker to take care of all his best interests. Peter's family's mistake was not keeping an eye on who was getting close to their relative. And it's an all too common predicament today.

Here also is some other of the top investment scams targeting the fifty plus market. The source of this information comes from John Nestor, director, public affairs, Securities and Exchange Commission, Washington, DC. He has been the investor education spokesman at the Commission since 1997. For more information see: *www.sec.gov*

Charitable Gift Annuities . . .

In this scheme, a fraudster poses as a staff member of a charitable organization. In exchange for a donation, he promises monthly annuity income for life at very attractive rates. Your donation will be invested to pay for an annuity, and also benefit the charity. Unbeknownst to the investor, payments are not invested for charitable purposes, but go directly to the fraudster's personal account. The charity doesn't exist; it's a front for the fraud.

Chances are the check will have to be made to the fraudster's charity. So check out the charity. This is a sample of custody, as we discussed above, as well. In annuity insurance product for the check would have to be made to an insurance company. Not to the charity.

High return or risk-free investment . . .

Scam artists often tout unrealistic returns or the lack of risk. Example: in one scheme, fraudsters induced more than 800 elderly investors nationwide to invest in a note that purportedly paid a guaranteed return of 5.5 percent to 8 percent. The fraudsters claim that investor's funds would be used to make the cure loans to businesses. They also represented that . . .

Independent administrators conducted due diligence on the notes.

Investors would be repaid their principal at maturity and/or . . .

Investors could redeem all or part of their investments before maturity, subject to a penalty.

All these representations were false. The investor's money was actually "Invested" in the fraudster's personal bank account.

Be wary of any opportunity that promises a stellar profits or "Guaranteed" returns. Find out if the product is an insurance product and therefore registered with your state insurance department or a securities product and/or registered with the SEC.

High return CDs . . .

Investors searching for relatively low risk investments that can easily be converted into cash often turn to bank certificates of deposit (CDs). Although most investors have traditionally purchased CDs through local banks, many brokerage firms now offer CDs. These brokerage firms, known as deposit brokers, can sometimes negotiate a higher rate of interest for a CD at a bank by promising to bring a certain amount of deposits to the institution. The deposit broker can then offer those brokered CDs to their customers passing along a higher rate of interest.

However, the SEC found that fraudsters posing as legitimate deposit brokers raised money by selling CDs that did not exist to fool unsuspecting investors. The names of the fake banks that many successful scams have used such as, "Chase Trust Bank," are very similar to the large legitimate banks that fraudsters distributed to shift investment documents and account statements to ensure that victims continue to invest in the scheme.

Be wary of above market returns offered through out of state banks. Victims are more likely to look at returns much higher than those offered by their local banks and will be inclined to believe that such returns from a bank in another state are legitimate. Make sure the bank is a legitimate bank or the custodian, who holds the CD, is a legitimate custodian.

Promissory notes . . .

A promissory note is a form of debt, similar to a loan or an IOU that a company may issue to raise money. Typically, an investor agrees to lend money to the company for a set period of time. In exchange, the company promises to pay the investor a fixed return (interest) on his/her investment, as well as return the principle. While promissory notes can be legitimate, those that are marketed broadly to older investors often turn out to be scams.

Example: the fraudsters purchased and used mailing list to target elderly individuals in Texas for investments in so-called "Guaranteed" and fully collateralized "Promissory notes." To set out even more bait for senior citizens, the fraudsters created alarm in this group by disseminating literature with claims that the Texas probate process was lengthy, complicated and expensive, and suggested that they could provide "A estate—planning services," "Living trust" and "Revocable trusts," to overcome this problem.

When the targets of the mailing responded, they were urged by the fraudsters to liquidate legitimate, safe investments, to withdraw IRA monies and to invest in high risk investments to achieve a higher rate of return. Investors were told their money would be used to fund business ventures, including short-term, high interest notes, bank cards, resort projects, and short-term interim mortgage loans—none of which existed.

The best self-defense is to seek the advice of your investment advisor or accountant when reviewing any potential investment opportunity. Always the wary of someone selling something that we discussed earlier.

Prime bank instruments . . .

With any so-called "Prime bank" scheme, fraudsters claim investors funds will be used to purchase and trade "Prime bank" financial instruments—a fictitious type of security—on overseas markets. The supposed objective is to generate huge returns in which the investors will share area. Neither these instruments, nor the market, on which they allegedly trade, exist.

The schemes seem legitimate—the promoters distribute documents that appear complex, sophisticated and official. The sellers frequently tell potential investors that they have special access to programs that otherwise would be reserved for top financiers on Wall Street, or in London, Geneva or other world financial centers. Investors are also promised a profit of 100 percent or more are possible, typically within a short timeframe, say, six months, with little risk.

After what happened in 2008, would you really want to do anything "Top financiers" would do? They can't even keep their own companies from going bankrupt.

An Advance Fee . . .

An advance fee fraud is a *confidence trick*, in which the target is persuaded to advance sums of money in the hope of realizing a significantly larger gain. Among the variations on this type of *scam*, are the Nigerian Letter (also called the 419 fraud, Nigerian scam, Nigerian bank scam, or Nigerian money offer).

This scam usually begins with a letter or e-mail purportedly sent to a selected recipient, but actually sent to many, making an offer that would result in a large payoff for the victim. The details vary, but the usual story is that a person, often a government or bank employee, knows of a large amount of unclaimed money or gold, which he cannot access directly, usually because he has no right to it.

Such people, who may be real, impersonated people, or fictitious characters played by the *con artist*, could include the wife or son of a deposed African or Indonesian leader or *dictator* who has amassed a stolen fortune, or a bank employee who knows of a terminally ill wealthy person with no relatives or a wealthy foreigner who deposited money in the bank just before dying in a plane crash (leaving no *will* or known *next of kin*), a US soldier who has stumbled upon a hidden cache of gold in Iraq, a business being audited by the government, a disgruntled worker or corrupt government official who has embezzled funds, a refugee, and similar characters.

The money could be in the form of *gold bullion*, gold dust, money in a bank account, *blood diamonds*, a series of checks or bank drafts, and so forth. The sums involved are usually in the millions of dollars, and the investor is promised a large share, typically ten to 40 percent, if they assist the scam character in retrieving the money.

Most people ignore these e-mails, but a very small percentage respond, enough to make the fraud worthwhile as many millions of messages can be sent. Invariably sums of money which are substantial, but very much smaller than the promised profits, are said to be required in advance for bribes, fees, etc.—this is the money being stolen from the victim, who thinks he or she is investing to make a huge profit.

I am hoping that if you have managed to get this far into a book on finances you are not the “Target market” for this type of scam, but it was too big to ignore.

A rule of thumb to use in virtually every situation is do you want to bet on the possibilities or the probabilities. Go with what is probable, not possible. For example, is it possible to get better returns playing in Las Vegas than it is investing in stocks? It is! However, it is highly improbable. Go with things where time and numbers are on your side.

The finish!

Truth is not Ice Cream, Faith is not Wishing

Greg Koukl, the President of Stand to Reason, has a speech that is titled, "Truth Is Not Ice Cream, Faith Is Not Wishing." Greg has a Masters in Philosophy of Religion and Ethics and writes and speaks extensively on clear thinking and how to defend truth claims. Even though this lecture was not specifically designed to deal with the truth claims I am making in this book, I will be borrowing heavily from his clear thinking.

Imagine you were watching an episode of Oprah. She came on the screen on a Monday afternoon, with great concern and said there was a national outbreak of small pox that was spreading very quickly and because of the reach of her program the government asked her to step in to get the word out. She explains the government got ahead of the crisis and is in the process of getting out an antidote that they have had for years and it is thoroughly tested. All they have to do is mass produce it and get it distributed to everyone. Since the antidote has been around for so long they have duplicate samples in virtually every major city and hundreds of labs have agreed to follow the strict, but simple and easy to follow guidelines to mass produce it. The government estimates by the end of the week everyone that wants the antidote, can get it. She says the bad news is that those that have to wait the full five days may feel some extreme discomfort, the good news, if they take the antidote they will not die. Now a word from our sponsors . . .

After coming back from the commercial she explains that her show has a long standing tradition of being open minded and she does not want to offend anyone with this singular strategy to avoid what "Could" be an uncomfortable experience and what "Could" result in death. So she has taken a poll and she came to the conclusion that the least uncomfortable solution is to eat ice cream instead. Everyone likes ice cream, there are enough flavors for every palate, and you will not have to wait to have it, you can pick some up on the way home from work. Besides, there are likely to be lines to get the antidote and there are far more locations that you can get ice cream. This will not offend anyone because there are lots of flavors and no one can be offended by someone's taste or preference in ice cream flavor.

Truth is not ice cream! It is not something that comes in multiple flavors. It is not a taste, it is not a preference. It is either true or it isn't. 2 + 2 always equals 4. You jump up you will come down regardless of how high you jumped. These things are true. To quote Greg Koukl, "When choosing ice cream, you can choose what you like. When choosing medicine, you must choose what heals. When choosing ice cream you can choose what's true for you. When choosing medicine you must choose what's true." You may prefer not to believe in math or gravity, but that does not change that they are true. I believe that the principles that are outlined in this book are medicine types of statements, not ice cream types of statements. If you ignore Financial Gravity, or the Diversity Trinity you do so at your own peril. TV, magazines and other media outlets are trying to compete for your dollars and they add lots of sugar to the poison that they are selling, but as the saying goes, all that glitters is not gold. The antidote to the poison you have ingested is the prudent, simple and disciplined approaches I have outlined. Simple, not easy. Timeless Wisdom, Strategic Application.

Many take what I have outlined and will have faith that it will work. I would rather they did not do that. The problem with the word, faith, is it is often combined with; leap of, or blind, and I have tried to make a reasoned defense of my strategies and tactics. Traditionally the word faith meant something different than what it means today. Faith historically was based on a logical order. First you acquired evidence, that evidence was tested which leads to knowledge. Then you trust (faith) that these logical steps have brought you to the right conclusions. I believe I have done this in the previous pages.

The proliferation of crime shows, two NCISs, the three CSIs, the countless Law and Order's, all show this logical progression. It is strange that there is such a huge desire for this type of programming when most of society rejects this logic in almost every aspect of their personal life. If nature abhors a vacuum, I suppose it makes sense that in a wealthy culture many fantasies thought unattainable just a few years ago are ours for the taking. So past fantasy is now present reality. This leads us to want more reality in our entertainment or fantasy. So fantasy has become reality requiring us to get reality in our fantasy. This would be a great book all by itself, but this discussion is about finances.

Many people have been able to accumulate great wealth as measured against the rest of the world and any time in history. We have lifestyles never dreamed of but, this fantasy life has led many to believe that the laws of the universe have been suspended; they haven't. If you want to maintain the fantasy life or have the fantasy life, you have to build and maintain it with time and discipline. Eating all the ice cream you can will make you fat and eventually kill you. It will please you momentarily, but the pleasure fades. Building your future with ice cream types of decisions will do the same, they please for a moment (tech bubble, Madoff, stock picking . . .) but the ride is temporary. Following the principles outlined in this book are like a good diet and exercise, they are simple, but not easy. They don't provide immediate pleasure; in fact, they require self control and discipline. But, when you take all the ingredients in this book and mix them together, you have the perfect recipe for a life and legacy of meaning.

ENDNOTES

1 Baker PHD, Dan, What Happy People Know, Rodale, 2003, pg 45-47

2 Slott, Ed, *The Retirement Savings Time Bomb . . . and How to Defuse It,* Penguin Books, 2003, pp xi.

3 CIPOM102005 powerpoint.

4 "Motive—definition," based on the Random House Unabridged Dictionary, Random House, Inc., November 2006.

5 Weiss, Joseph W., "Motivation, Learning, and Rewards," page 82, Organization Behavior & Change, West Publishing Company, 1996.

6 Yeager, Joseph, "Databases Don't Measure Motivation," Sommer Consulting Inc., Nova Southeastern, *http://www.nova.edu/ssss/QR/QR10-1/yeager.pdf,* 2005.

7 Yeager, Joseph, "Databases Don't Measure Motivation," Sommer Consulting Inc., Nova Southeastern, *http://www.nova.edu/ssss/QR/QR10-1/yeager.pdf,* 2005.

8 Moneyinstructor.com, "4 Budget Pitfalls to Avoid."

9 Moneyinstructor.com, "Reasons Budgets Fail."

10 Keating, Peter, "The Second Time Around," *SmartMoney Magazine*, February 2009, pg 42-43.

11 Slott, pp 34.

12 Slott, pp 35-38.

13 Slott, pp 23-24.

14 Slott, pp 30.

15 T.Rowe Brokerage, "A Lifetime Investment Solution," *T.Rowe Investor*, December 2008, pg 14.

16 Extension.org, "What is the Earnings Limits for Social Security?" FAQ #27517, Extension.org, *http://www.extension.org/faq/27517*, accessed February 7, 2009.

17 Koukl, Greg, STRs The Page—August 2009

18 "Top Things to Know—Debt," CNNMoney.com, Money, *http://www.cnnmoney.com*, November 2006

19 Allebrand, Cheryl, "Tallying the True Costs of Debt," Bankrate.com, *http://www.bankrate.com/brm/news/financial_literacy/debt_management/cost_of_debt_a1.asp*, accessed December 21, 2008

20 Allebrand, Cheryl "Tallying the True Costs of Debt." Bankrate.com

21 Bucci, Steve, "The Top 10 Causes of Debt," Bankrate.com, May 1, 2006, *http://www.bankrate.com/brm/green/debt-consolidation/basics1-3a.asp?caret=4*, accessed December 21, 2008.

22 Adapted from Cannon Financial Institute Concepts for Professionals, A Complete Library of Essential Financial Concepts, 2001 pp108-111

23 "Budgeting Money & Debt: Inflow vs. Outflow," MoneyInstructor.com, Money Instructor, 2005.

24 Scott, pp 3.

25 Investorwords, "Basis points-definition," investorwords.com, February 6, 2009, *http://www.investorwords.com/434/basis_point.html*

26 Cruz, Humberto, "Mutual Industry Isn't Telling You What You Need to Know on Fees," Arizona Daily Star, March 24, 2004

27 Bogle, John C., "The Little Book of Common Sense Investing" John Wiley & Sons, 2007 pg. xvi

28 Bogle, John C., pg. xvii

29 D'Arruda, Peter J. "Fine Print Fiasco*" pp 87-91

30 D'Arruda, Peter J. "Fine Print Fiasco*" pp 87-91

31 Goodman, Beverly, "Parents in Crisis," SmartMoney Magazine, February 2009, pg 73.

32 "Top Things to Remember—Financial Planner," CNNMoney.com, Money, *http://www.cnnmoney.com*, November 2006

33 Orman, Suze, "The Five Signs of Bad Financial Advice," Money Matters, *http://finance.yahoo.com/columnist/article/moneymatters/11727?p=1*, November 6, 2006.

34 Orman, Suze, Money Matters.

35 Orman, Suze, Money Matters.

36 Kingdom Advisors Training, Session 15, page 2

37 Bhaktavatsalam, Sree, "Fidelity, Franklin Stick Investors with Tax Bills as Funds Fall," Bloomberg.com, December 1, 2008, accessed December 2, 2008.

38 Slott, pp 203-204.

39 Slott, pp 208.

40 Slott, pp 209-210.

41 Scott, pp 3.

42 Kingdom Advisors Training, Session 15, page 5

43 Pollock, John, "Advanced IRA Slides," powerpoint, April 2008.

44 http://en.wikipedia.org/wiki/Vetting

45 Swift, Marie, Is Modern Portfolio Dead, Published in the 5/1/2009 Issue of Research Magazine.

46 Matson, Michelle, *Rich Chick,* 2009, pg 104.

47 T.Rowe Brokerage, "Following Your Plan in Volatile Markets," *T.Rowe Investor*, December 2008, pg 11.

48 Lewin, C G (1970). "An Early Book on Compound Interest-Richard Witt's Arithmetical Questions." *Journal of the Institute of Actuaries* 96 (1): 121-132.

49 Lewin, C G (1981). "Compound Interest in the Seventeenth Century." *Journal of the Institute of Actuaries* 108 (3): 423-442.

50 http://www.isa.org/Content/ContentGroups/InTech2/Features/20023/September8/20020938.pdf

51 After the Crash, Abundance Technologies, powerpoint 10/2008

52 http://www.bloomberg.com/apps/news?pid=20601203&sid=aw2cpNsLMXqg

53 http://en.wikipedia.org/wiki/Amusing_Ourselves_to_Death

54 Examining Your Expectations, McGriff Video Productions pg 8

55 Examining Your Expectations, McGriff Video Productions pg 9

56 Examining Your Expectations, McGriff Video Productions pg 13

57 http://en.wikiquote.org/wiki/Heraclitus

58 Orman, Suze, *Suze Orman's 2009 Action Plan,* Spiegel & Grau, New York, 2009, pg 188.

59 Orman, pg 189.

60 Os Guinness, *The Call,* (Nashville, W Publishing Group, 1998) pg 1.

61 Slott, pp 176.

62 Slott, pp 177.

63 Keating, pg 36-37.

64 Slott, pp 159.

65 Motley Fool Staff, "Your Life Insurance Number," Yahoo News section, Yahoo!, The Motley Fool, *http://news.yahoo.com/s/fool/20061024/bs_fool_fool/116171355713*, October 24, 2006.

66 Slott, pp 156.

67 Adapted from Kingdom Advisors Training, Session 17, page 2

68 Adapted from Kingdom Advisors Training, Session 17, page 2

Index

A

B

C

D

E

J

K

L

M

N

O

P

Q

R

S

T

V

W

To learn more...

...visit us

www.johnpollock.tv

Hundreds of video episodes—Blog with me daily

...follow us

John Pollock's Journal E-newsletter

Receive weekly updates and good news in the marketplace

To sign up, go to www.johnpollock.tv and click on "Subscribe" under "Subscribe to E-Newsletter."

JohnPollock.tv Blog

Receive John Pollock's weekly blogs at a glance.

To sign up, go to www.johnpollock.tv and enter your email address under "Subscribe to Blog"

facebook

Facebook.com/johnpollock

Twitter.com/johnpollockinc

Edwards Brothers, Inc.
Thorofare, NJ USA
January 25, 2012